The Rector
Who Wouldn't
Pray for Rain

By the same author:

A Parish Adult Education Handbook – Editor

Believe It Or Not – A Memoir

That Could Never Be – with K. Dalton

The Rectory Dog – Poetry Collection

The Rector
Who
Wouldn't
Pray for Rain

Patrick Semple

MERCIER PRESS
WHAT YOU NEED TO READ

MERCIER PRESS
Douglas Village, Cork
www.mercierpress.ie

Trade enquiries to Columba Mercier Distribution,
55a Spruce Avenue, Stillorgan Industrial Park, Blackrock, Dublin

© Patrick Semple, 2007

978 1 85635 560 5

10 9 8 7 6 5 4 3 2 1

Excerpt from 'New Hampshire' from *The Poetry of Robert Frost* edited by Edward Connery Lathem. Copyright 1923, 1969 by Henry Holt and Company. Copyright 1951 by Robert Frost. Reprinted by permission of Henry Holt and Company, LLC.
The lines from Patrick Kavanagh's 'Lough Derg' are reprinted from *Collected Poems*, edited by Antoinette Quinn (Allen Lane, 2004) by kind permission of the Trustees of the Estate of the late Katherine B. Kavanagh, through the Jonathan Williams Literary Agency.

Mercier Press receives financial assistance from
the Arts Council/An Chomhairle Ealaíon

Printed and bound by J.H. Haynes & Co. Ltd, Sparkford.

Contents

For Shane and Amy

'You might as well ask the paralytic to leap from his chair, and throw away his crutch, or, without a miracle, to "take up his bed and walk", as expect the learned reader to throw down his book and think for himself.'

WILLIAM HAZLITT, 'On the Ignorance of the Learned'

Acknowledgments

I would like to thank Michael Burrows for reading the manuscript and for making helpful suggestions and Patricia Jeffares, Cyril Nolan, Georgina Rothwell and Hilary Semple for help willingly given.

Some names have been changed to protect anonymity.

Preface

In *Believe it or Not*, published in 2002, I tried to give some insight into what it was like to be brought up in the 1940s and 1950s in the tiny Protestant community in the Republic of Ireland, a minority that was less than 5 per cent of the population. I went on to give an insider view of the Church of Ireland based on my own experience in the ministry, and to show something of the development of inter-church relations at parish level in Ireland after the Second Vatican Council. As a subtext to all of this I mentioned my own difficulties with belief in the Christian faith.

Of course another Protestant brought up at the same time might have given a slightly different perspective, but I believe I represented fairly the main attitudes and beliefs and the overall atmosphere that prevailed in the minority community. Shortly after the book was published I had a letter from another Church of Ireland clergyman who had been a student in college at the same time that I was there, but whose theological position was poles apart from mine. He confirmed that his experience of growing up in Drogheda over the same period and his time in the ministry were uncannily similar to my own.

I am confident that my account of growing up in the tiny Church of Ireland community in Wexford was largely speaking, in day-to-day terms, representative of the Church of Ireland in the south of Ireland as a whole, and my experience in the ministry was representative too. The first sentence of my colleague's letter, however, was: 'Since we never saw eye to eye you will be surprised to hear from me.' This illustrates the diversity of theological opinion I mentioned in *Believe it or Not* that exists within Anglicanism which is the theological position of the Church of Ireland; a diversity of theological interpretation within a common doctrinal base. My former student colleague was conservative, evangelical and relied primarily on revelation while I was liberal, broad church and according to him relied primarily on reason. Roman Catholics, I believe, do not generally understand this diversity within Anglicanism.

After the publication of *Believe it or Not* a number of people, however, said things like: 'You should have told us more about your childhood … Why did you not say more about your time in Belfast? … You didn't tell us enough about your doubts and what you actually believe.' Here I expand on these and on some other topics.

I have always been conscious that Roman Catholics of my generation understood Protestantism from what they were taught in their religion classes in school at a time when ecumenism was non-existent. Many told me later that this was in fact the case. They were taught that outside the Church there is no salvation, and 'the Church' was deemed to be the Roman Catholic Church. This meant simply that Protestants automatically go to hell, and Catholics were often taught this explicitly. This was a time when it was a sin for a Roman Catholic to enter a Protestant church during a service. For example, in 1949 the Taoiseach, John Costello, and his government, with the exception of Noel Browne, waited in their cars near St Patrick's Cathedral during the funeral service of Douglas Hyde the former President of the country. Either they did not ask permission to attend the service or they asked permission and it was refused. Talking about this with a friend, a Catholic priest, recently he claimed that the ban on Catholics attending Protestant services resulted from Protestant clergy trying to convert Roman Catholics in the past. This came as a surprise to me since in my lifetime I never came across an attempt to convert anyone from Catholicism in church, nor a word in criticism of Catholicism. In this instance the clergy conducting the funeral service of a former President of Ireland would hardly use the opportunity to proselytise Catholics. I have no doubt there are certain kinds of Protestants who would try at the drop of a hat to convert Catholics and Catholics are right to stay away from their services. Where Catholics try to convert Protestants, the Protestant Churches do not lay down rules but leave such matters to the free conscience of the individual.

The case of the Taoiseach and the funeral of Douglas Hyde is a far cry from the recent situation in which a Catholic Archbishop of Dublin appealed to Church of Ireland clergy not to invite Roman Catholics to receive communion in Church of Ireland churches. The Protestant mind inevitably questions what has changed. Why the change from the tight control of the Church at the time of the Douglas Hyde funeral to the recent loss of control over Catholics receiving communion in Church of Ireland churches? I will try to say here how Roman Catholicism in general appears from the Protestant perspective.

Roman Catholic friends have told me over the years that they did not distinguish between the different Protestant Churches. Much of what they were told in school seems to have been about the Church of Ireland and this is understandable since the Anglican Church indirectly imposed the draconian Penal Laws on Catholics. As I understand it some of what was taught about the Church of Ireland in Catholic schools was either half true or false, bearing in mind that a half-truth is often worse than a falsehood. For example, that Henry VIII started the Church of Ireland; that he founded a new Church in the sixteenth century and that the Church of Ireland does not believe in the Virgin Mary. These are either half-truths or they are false. I did not set out to develop the Church of Ireland theological position on these matters in *Believe it or Not* but I will mention them here in a way, I hope, will be clear to the average lay person.

I am not a theologian. Most theologians are bright, intelligent academics who teach in seminaries or universities. Many of them are ordained in one Christian tradition or another and a few are lay people. Most are practising Christians, which perhaps calls into question the objectivity of some of their conclusions. Maybe we should have some theologians of Christianity that are not Christians. It was theologians in earlier times who agonised over how many angels could dance on the head of a pin. Before they embarked on this nonsense did they demonstrate that angels existed in the first place? Perhaps theologians today have moved on but is it possible that their concerns today are equally abstract and remote from the daily lives and religious concerns of the person in the street? I believe that theology is only valid when it takes account of the day-to-day lives of ordinary people and includes a contribution from them. Theology that emanates from the halls of academia or the corridors of power of the institutional Churches alone must be suspect. It is interesting to note, in passing, that in ordinary language today the word 'theological' is often used to mean 'abstract gobbledygook!'

I am distinctly uncomfortable with much of what I believe to be the abstract speculation of academic theology, however I will touch on some theological issues in such a way that I hope they will be easily understood by lay people. I was once averagely theologically literate but I have forgotten much of it. I do however know where to find again those bits that I want to use, especially those bits that will reinforce me in my own prejudices!

There are volumes of weighty theological tomes written on the topics that will only be mentioned here, few, if any, of which I have read and even if I were to read them it would be a struggle for me to understand half of them. I became fed up reading theology after about thirty-five years when it finally dawned on me that not only was I not finding answers to my questions, but that I was ending up with more questions than when I started. I decided to abandon my hope of finding someone to answer my questions and decided, rightly or wrongly, to make up my own mind; to do my own theology. There is of course a case to be made for serious academic theology, and I do not support the view that all theologians should be made to go and get themselves a proper job. Although maybe some should.

In *Believe it or Not* I gave a picture of what the Church of Ireland was like from the inside, against which Roman Catholics could test their own image of this tiny minority in the south. A thread will run through this book of how from within this small community I, and I believe Church of Ireland people generally, saw the large Roman Catholic community whose Church dominated society as a whole. You will note that I use the past tense; I do this consciously as I will be talking mainly about the past in Ireland. Things have changed so much recently and are still changing so fast religiously in Irish society that I will only mention some of the most recent developments. I will also address more directly what was a subtext in *Believe it or Not*, namely my own difficulties with Christian belief. I will try to set out honestly where these difficulties have brought me today and I will do all of this in the context of ordinary everyday life.

Memory is selective. Have you ever experienced being with a group of people with whom you were at school many years before when the 'Do you remembers' start? 'Do you remember so and so?' 'Do you remember the day that ...' What is fascinating about these occasions is the incidents that people remember of which others have no memory. Perhaps we remember the incidents that were interesting or amusing for us and forget those that were unpleasant or painful.

It is clear that for one reason or another individual memory is selective. I think it is true to say too that our memories are also affected by the 'good old days' factor. Those of us who are old enough remember things that mark us out as venerable; fair days on the streets, valve radios and milk delivered from the farm into your own jug at the door, things that have gone for good in this affluent, electronic and hygienic world in which we live today. A.N.Wilson has said about the selectivity of memory:

> The power of total recall is never vouchsafed, not even to the most vivid imaginations or intellects. In our personal mythologies we select a very few characters and incidents to masquerade, in memory or half-memory, as our past.

These last observations are a prelude to some more memories of childhood in Wexford Town where I was born and brought up. It is because people seem to have been fascinated by those memories and said they would like to hear more that I am bold enough to inflict some more upon anyone who is interested to read on. There is something about returning to where you were brought up many years after you have left and remembering your time as a child with people who have lived there continuously during the intervening fifty or so years. You find that you have carried with you during your absence some people and events that those who have lived there continuously have forgotten.

Much more importantly however, these selective memories provide the backdrop against which I grew up and became aware of the world and my questions about God and religion. These questions have been with me in one shape or form from the time I was old enough to reflect upon them and in a more developed way many of them are still with me today.

If you think I am going to answer all the questions I pose, or all the questions that you may have, you might as well put this book down now and spend your time more profitably wallpapering the bedroom or digging the garden. You may, however, be prepared to acknowledge all the good things about the Christian faith, take them for granted and leave them aside for the moment and look at the times Christian Churches and Church leaders failed to live up to the Gospel. You may be prepared to look at some of the problems for Christian belief and come with me to look at areas where I am sometimes out of my depth. If so keep reading and perhaps someone else will enlighten us on some of these matters and provide us with some satisfactory answers, or maybe they won't.

1

The Town

My earliest memories, strangely enough, are of people other than my family. I remember well our neighbours who lived in the houses on either side of us on the terrace at the top of Hill Street where I was born and where I lived until I was six. I have memories of them and of events outside my home more clearly than I have memories of my home and family.

There were the Howlins; three girls and a boy. Peggy had a calliper on one leg that caused me to wonder at the connection when I first saw a stick of 'Peggy's leg' in a sweet shop. One day out of the blue one of the Howlin girls proffered the information to the rest of us that she was going to be a nun. One of her sisters informed her authoritatively that you couldn't just be a nun you had to have a vocation. What that was I had not the remotest idea, but the implication was that the prospective postulant, whatever it was, had not got such a thing.

There were the Whelans. During the war Mr Whelan was the senior member of the LDF, the part-time Local Defence Force in which my father served. It was the Irish version of 'Dad's Army!' I'm not sure what they did but they trained at something and marched on formal occasions. As far as I remember they wore a navy blue uniform and some years after the war a Garda arrived at our door with a service medal for my father. He was embarrassed at receiving a medal for doing so little and put it away in a drawer. One of his brothers had seen action through the North Africa campaign and into Italy where he was taken prisoner and spent the end of the war in a POW camp in Germany and another brother had been decorated for wartime military intelligence. I'm sure my father never told either of them, or anybody else for that matter, about his 'Dad's Army' medal. I know he was proud of the LDF and proud to have done what little he could; it would have been a matter of principle with him as a citizen to play his part.

Mrs Cleary and her son Richard, who was my first friend, lived in the end house at the top. There was no Mr Cleary. Mrs Cleary took in lodgers two of whom worked on the building of the new Presentation School on John's Road. There were Mr and Mrs Latimer and their only son Hugh, who was much older than I was, perhaps in his early teens, and a big lump of a lad. Mr Latimer was manager of the Cinema Palace in Cinema Lane. When I went there when I was older to Saturday matinees to see Roy Rogers, Gene Autrey and 'Hopalong' Cassidy he didn't recognise me as he stood with stern countenance beside the box office. We had moved house by then and I suppose I had changed or perhaps it was that in those days adults, especially men, did not speak to children. Mr and Mrs Conneely lived below us; Mr Conneely taught in the Technical School on Jail Road where my father went to evening classes in woodwork to build a case to house the movement of a grandfather clock that he insisted on calling a longcase clock. At the end of the back gardens of our terrace there was a lane that ran down from Bents, the first house around the corner on John Street. To me there was a great mystery about the Bents because I used to hear their voices over the tall hedge but never saw them. I had no faces to put with the voices and wouldn't have known them if I passed them on the street.

Opposite and a little further down Hill Street there was a terrace of houses where there were a lot of children who played out on the street. Nobody ever told me not to, but we never mixed with them and I have no doubt they were considered our social inferiors. Occasionally when we came and went they shouted threats across at us. Down the street on our side was Croke Avenue where I went only once, sent on a message to Mr Colfer the sweep to come to sweep the chimney. His hands and face were black and he walked smartly carrying his brushes on his shoulder.

Hopkins grocery shop was at the top of John Street. It was important in the lives of local children, as it was the nearest shop that sold sweets. Mr Hopkins, a thickset man, wore a white coat. He was voluble, but dealt quickly with children while he continued his conversation with some housewife. I always felt my own simple transactions were a nuisance to him and an interruption to the important business of his shop – to keep up with local gossip, Irish news and affairs of the world at large. The talk was like men's barbershop talk where on one occasion I learned, while propped up on a box in the chair having a short back and sides, that without the Russians the Allies would never have won the war. Such weighty subjects were discussed with the same gravitas as the county's Sunday hurling victory in Wexford Park.

Walsh's Pub was along the footpath from Hopkins. It was a sober looking premises, painted black, with the name in gold paint over the door. I don't remember seeing customers coming or going, but I suppose their main business was conducted after I had gone to bed. I have a feeling that their clientele was regular and select; a cut above that of the average pub. It looked like premises on which it is hard to believe a serious disagreement between customers ever took place or on which a song was ever sung. It was the home of Dr Tom Walsh who in due course, as a result of his interest in opera, founded the Wexford Festival. His sister Nellie was a noted singer and my parents used to listen to the wireless when she broadcast on Radio Éireann. She was a tall woman, or so she seemed to me, who smiled readily and always talked warmly to us children if we said 'hello' to her first.

Further up John Street at Wygram there was a monument to Charles Valloton. In 1793, according to a wall plaque in St Iberius Church of Ireland church, 'when zealously co-operating with the civil power in support of the mild and beneficent laws of his country, he received a mortal wound from a savage hand', a rebel of one kind or another. The 'civil power' erected the monument to his memory. He was obviously a member of the Protestant ruling class of the time when the Corporation of Wexford was composed of members of his own kind. The inscription on the wall tablet in St Iberius, however, gives no hint that he is believed to have struck the first blow himself, unprovoked, and the 'savage hand' was acting in self defence and obviously to great effect. There was a horse trough beside the monument at which young boys played and filled with all kinds of rubbish.

Opposite the monument and trough there was a private garage that gave access to the garden of Dr George and Dr Helen Hadden, husband and wife, retired lay Methodist medical missionaries who had spent many years in China. They lived around the corner at Wygram, and the garden of their house extended to here. During the war my father rented a portion of their garden to grow vegetables. Apart from the piece he cultivated the rest of the garden was largely neglected. When I went there with him when he was working, I used to wander into the fruit garden (which was forbidden territory) to where I could not be seen and eat some of the biggest, ripest and sweetest gooseberries I have ever come across. I have never had gooseberries like them since.

In the garage there was a Morris 8 motor car up on blocks for the duration of the war in which I used to go on fascinating journeys at breakneck speed while my father was working to keep the family in vegetables. As I write I can smell the leather upholstery of that temporarily retired motor. After the war Dr Helen drove it around town and no doubt further afield, but never as expertly or as fast as I had done when it was up on blocks. She once gave me a lift from Avenue de Flandres to the Bull Ring and handed me her huge ear trumpet to mind while she drove. She explained to me that she was always glad when a pedestrian was crossing the end of a street she was passing as it indicated to her that no car was coming down that street on a collision course with her. I felt it polite to respond to what she was saying but she couldn't hear a word I said as her ear trumpet was on my knee. Dr Helen couldn't reverse. When she called on a particular friend on Spawell Road she had to continue as far as Carcur and turn right back to town, doing a circuit to get home.

Dr George was a civic-minded man who was the only Protestant on Wexford Corporation at the time. He rode a bicycle which had a motor fitted on the back carrier with a drive to the back wheel. He didn't use the motor going down town as it was all downhill. He was a big man and he put the motor to the test as it 'put put putted' up Hill Street on his way home.

A woman of an authoritarian and determined temperament who wasn't keen on children playing near her house lived nearby the Valloton monument. One hot summer day when the heat melted the tar macadam joints on the paving, one of the children, knowing she was not at home, made balls of the tar and put them into the can of milk at her door. The milkman, a farmer from out the country, who smelled of stale milk, came to town every day with a horse and cart and churn. He would decant the milk into a smaller can and deliver it from door to door. He knocked quickly along a row of three or four houses and then went back to the first one, so he would not have to wait too long for each door to open. He would 'hup, hup' the horse to keep it coming along the street to be beside him when he finished the row. At each door he poured from the can into a pint measure and into the housewife's jug, always with a tilly for the cat, whether there was a cat or not, sometimes splashing the step with milk to the annoyance of the housewife. It wasn't in his interest to waste milk or in the housewife's to have a dirty step, but the clean transfer of milk from measure to jug required no small skill and practice. If there was nobody at home a can with lid, or a jug with saucer on top was left for the milkman on the doorstep, leaving the milk vulnerable to predatory cats and dogs and to contamination on hot summer days from balls of tar macadam dropped in by children.

Hadden's milkman, in order to speed up his round, was training a boy to help. Early in his career the youngster rang on Hadden's bell and when Dr Helen answered the door, the better to hear the somewhat timid apprentice milkman she put her ear trumpet down in front of him, into which he delivered the contents of his pint measure.

Hill Street was a main route to Wexford GAA Park so that on the Sunday of a big match crowds trooped up the hill past our house. They were mainly men, and many of them from the country pushed big Raleigh or Rudge bicycles and if the weather was fine they had their coats tied over the handlebars. When the match started, I could hear the cheers from the Park from our back garden to which I was confined to observe the quietness of a Protestant Sunday. I would play an imaginary match of my own until I heard the supporters coming down again when I was allowed out to the front door to ask if Wexford had won.

This was the mid 1940s, the days before marts when on fair day, once a month, farmers brought pigs, sheep and cattle to town to sell. Without any say in the matter townies handed over some of their streets to these swarthy men and their animals for a long and busy day. Farmers drove their stock many miles in the small hours of the morning to arrive early and secure the most favourable pitches. The fair was held in our part of town and we were woken early by the sound of cattle on the street outside. It was an exciting day for a small boy and it gave me a glimpse of a life about which I knew nothing.

The farmer kept his cattle under control on the street by facing them to the wall and standing behind them, ash plant in hand, ready to tap on the rump any animal that might think of turning round. Occasionally a beast would take advantage of a lapse in concentration and bolt for it. It would career down the middle of the street, only to be stopped by a farmer further down standing, legs apart, arms extended, making as much noise as he could with his stick on the ground and 'hup, hup, hupping' at the top of his voice. When the beast saw there was no way through it was driven back to stand again facing the wall like a dunce.

Farmers transported pigs: sows, bonamhs (piglets) and sometimes a boar in creel carts drawn by an ass or a jennet and pulled the cart in at right angles to the footpath. They unyoked the ass or jennet from between the shafts, propped them up, and brought the animal to one of the yards at Westgate or North Main Street to stable it for the day. Pigs often fell asleep and an interested buyer would poke them through the creels to stand them up, the better to inspect them. Some farmers were entrusted by their wives with fowl or eggs to sell, no doubt with strict instructions as to price and in some cases with dire warnings not to drink the proceeds. A cow brought to town for sale might have to be milked and some lucky townie housewife would receive a present of a pail of milk to cool and strain and share with neighbours.

There was a ritual to the buying and selling of a beast. The purpose of this ritual was for the buyer to get the owner to reduce his inflated view of the value of his animal and for the seller to convince the buyer to increase his lesser estimate of its worth. The prospective buyer would survey the beast from all angles to see if the critical points for its development were good and to evaluate if it would fit into his scheme of things at home. If it was still a possibility he might poke the animal to confirm his judgement. At this early stage neither would show his hand, but each would manoeuvre himself into the most advantageous position in which to offer tentatively the possibility of negotiation. A price would be mentioned as a starter and the ritual would begin, both employing every ruse possible to achieve their own price. This involved offers and rejections and when the difference had been reduced to make a deal look possible there was much spitting on hands and walking away, when a third party might be brought in to broker the deal. Eventually one or other, or more likely both, would compromise and the sale was sealed with the spit on the palm, the handshake and the return of the luck penny. Many's the farmer, however, brought home, unsold, a beast because he didn't get his price, having stood for a long day at the fair.

As the day wore on a farmyard smell hung heavily over the streets and animal sounds left nobody in any doubt that the country had come to town. Women on their way to shop or the working man going home for lunch kept to the middle of the street, careful to avoid what in a field would be a tidy cowpat but on the street was a dispersal of a yard or more in all directions. This was the kind of thing farmers took for granted but that scandalised townies. Should this natural function occur while he passed, the townie was quick to take evasive action and looked not to a farmer but to another townie to share his outrage as though the beast should have held on until it got home.

Some of these bronzed and rugged people who came to town did their business and went home. Others made a day of it no matter what. They had lunch, some in pubs where there was nothing equivalent to what we know today as a pub lunch, while others went to Mernagh's Restaraunt or Love's Café, both on the Main Street near the Bull Ring.

There was an agricultural buzz in the town and it was good for trade, especially on the North Main Street. Shopkeepers took advantage of fair day. Hardware merchants displayed spades, forks, turnip grinders, barbed wire and bags of seed on the footpath outside their shops. They were amused but prepared for the farmers who haggled over their purchase in the same way they would for a beast. Drapery shops hung clothes outside their doors and shoe shops displayed wellingtons and hobnailed boots on stands or on the footpath outside. Farmers knew quality from the inferior item when it came to clothing and footwear. They felt the quality of the material or flexed the boot, for anything they bought would be tested in all weathers and in the kind of rough conditions townies could hardly imagine.

By late afternoon the business of the fair and the shopping had been done and most of the farmers had set out for home. The fire brigade came out and hosed down the streets to remove all traces of this rural invasion and return them to their rightful tenants for another month.

After the war we moved from Hill Street to the Main Street to live over my father's business – Richards, Jewellers. The house was a four storey Georgian townhouse the front of the ground floor of which was the shop. At the back was the disused flag-floored kitchen with cast-iron range. The old kitchen was now a dump room for anything that might or might not come in handy in the future and a park for the bicycles of the men in the workshop. The drawing room, dining room and kitchen were on the first floor and the bedrooms and bathroom were off a long corridor on the second floor, and over that the attic. Most of the attic rooms contained things that were fascinating to a small boy, from a tea chest full of the discarded movements of defunct watches to gas masks and piles of old Geographic Magazines. Later on I smuggled some of these magazines out to give them to a boy who fascinated me because he had an uncle who was younger than him.

From the drawing room windows we looked out on the Bull Ring and 'The Man' – the bronze monument of a pikeman commemorating the United Irishmen's rising of 1798. Behind him the meat market, down the side of which ran Common Quay Street, invariably pronounced Common 'Kay' Street, leading to the quay, invariably pronounced correctly. The Bull Ring was the focal point of the town. It was where events took place; political meetings at election time; where travelling salesmen set up their pitches when they came to town; and where Lizzie Meyler conducted her business on Fridays.

In those days trading on the streets was the most natural thing in the world, but somehow plying their trade on the street gained a reputation for fishwives as loud-mouthed women, and gave that meaning to the word in the English language. Why women who sold fish gained this reputation more than those who sold anything else I do not know.

Wexford had a notable fishwife, who, though her son was a successful fish merchant with a substantial business, wasn't too proud to sell fish from a cart every Friday. Jamesie Meyler bought fish from the local trawler men on the quay and from the boats in Rosslare and Kilmore and sent it all over the country. He wore a beige coloured Crombie overcoat, drove a fine motorcar and probably hadn't handled a fish in years. Lizzie, his mother, propped up the shafts of her cart on two fish boxes at the side of Traynor's hardware shop in the Bull Ring, facing down North Main Street. She sold herrings to all who felt constrained to observe the rule of their Church to abstain from meat on Fridays. Lizzie of course sold fish to anybody without fear or favour including members of the Church of Ireland, the rules of whose Church, whether they knew it or not, specified as days of fasting or abstinence 'all the Fridays in the year, except Christmas Day.' They didn't specify how this fasting or abstinence should be observed. I suspect Protestants ate fish on Fridays, not for religious reasons, but to vary their diet on the day the best and freshest fish was available.

Lizzie set up stall at about nine in the morning as the town began to stir and made her presence felt with: 'Herrinds, fresh herrinds' at the top of her voice. She was determined that nobody should be unaware of her presence, and she exchanged repartee with anybody who would engage with her and with the challenge of 'fresh herrinds, missus' to any passing woman whose eye she could catch.

She sold only herrings. The cart was full and according to herself they were so fresh they didn't yet know they were caught. People bought them by the half dozen and some asked for the female fish because they liked the roe and would cook it separately. To tell the male from the female Lizzie pressed her thumbs, one at either side of the small aperture underneath the fish near the tail to see if the female roe or the slimy sperm of the male emerged. She wrapped the fish in newspaper and handed them to the customer with a comment to the effect that there were never fish the likes of them.

From our drawing room windows we could see the corner-boys who stood against the New Ireland Assurance building at the corner of Cornmarket facing up the Main Street. This 'stand' gave them a view straight ahead as far as the end of Rowe Street or beyond and to their left they could keep the Bull Ring under surveillance. They were seasoned observers of the passing scene and had their finger on the pulse of the town itself. Like work, rain and cold are inimical to the vocation of cornerboy, so in bad weather they simply weren't there and were indistinguishable from the rest of the population. In moderately cold weather they might stick it out for a while, keeping warm as best they could, by moving from one foot to the other and by the occasional strenuous bout of flinging their arms around themselves. In warm sunny weather they came into their own. They were relaxed and conversation flowed. We could hear them from the open window. Flowed is not quite the word, for a subject never really got going before one of them would make a definitive statement designed to be the last word on the subject and to establish the speaker as the world authority on the matter. In really warm weather they would decamp to sit at the foot of 'The Man' and with their backsides contribute further to the polishing of the limestone base.

These cornerboys were all of an age, unemployed and wore hats or caps. There were no young men. It seemed that to be part of this elite club a man had to be of mature years. Occasionally a younger person or maybe a child would arrive bringing a message from home to one of the members who would leave to fulfil some family responsibility. On dole day there was a notable air of affluence about them: they smoked full length cigarettes out of a packet and there was much more coming and going than usual; trips to Con Macken's bar on the corner or down Common Quay Street to Corcoran's bookies on the quay.

In those days men, apart from trawler men, were almost never seen in public wearing just a sweater. Men always wore a jacket and often a waistcoat or maybe a pullover; so too for these gentlemen of leisure. Neither did they appear in public without a hat or cap, which they lifted, not for a passing lady, but for the Angelus or for a passing funeral. They were nothing if not religious. As soon as the sound of the first strike of the Angelus came from Rowe Street off came the hats and caps to reveal a variety of hairstyles and lack of them. Bobby Hughes, a hunchback, was a surprise: he was as bald as a coot and his pate was snow white, having had minimal exposure to the sun. Bobby looked much better with his cap on. Another had a surprisingly thick shock of grey hair and all of them looked different with their heads uncovered. They also removed hats and caps for a funeral passing through the Bull Ring from Bride Street or Rowe Street on its way to the cemetery at Crosstown. There was also the occasional funeral from the Church of Ireland church, St Iberius or the Methodist or Presbyterian church. When these passed, I have wondered since, did they think: 'Another poor Protestant on his way to eternal damnation.'

At election time political parties used the Bull Ring for election meetings in the evenings. They positioned a lorry where Lizzy Meyler sold her herrings on Fridays and erected loudspeakers on lampposts. This preparation was all done early on in the evening after the shops had closed and everything was in place ready. The politicians outlined, in their own modest way, what they had achieved in the past and listed all the marvellous things they would achieve for Ireland and her people, and particularly for the people of Wexford, when they were elected.

The speeches didn't start before nine o'clock and even then not until there was a reasonable number of people standing around. The cornerboys stood on their usual corner as though these places were reserved. I have no doubt they were more comfortable during the day when people passed by and resented this invasion of their territory. The noise from the loudspeakers attracted more people and in due course the complement was made up when the pubs closed. When the politicians started to speak they seemed to suffer from the delusion that the louder they shouted the more likely it was that their audience would believe them, and the longer they went on the more credible they would become. Even at the back of our house with doors and windows closed we were assailed until well after children's bedtime by political spiel and invective. On the following day when the lorry and loudspeakers had gone the litter on the street left nobody in any doubt that there had been a meeting there the night before.

The only other place I remember a political meeting in the town was at the Old Pound where there was a natural platform – the landing at the top of the steps on the outside of Cousins mineral water factory. I remember Brendan Corish, who I'm almost certain my parents always voted for, speaking at a meeting there. He lived near us at the far end of St Ibar's Terrace when we lived on Hill Street.

On nights that my parents went out Mrs Scanlon came in to baby-sit. Her husband died not long after the war and as was the custom with widows she dressed entirely in black with skirt to her ankles. Mr Scanlon had served in three wars; the Boer war and the two world wars. Two of her sons, clever boys, had worked for my father and another was work shy, but teased us children in the way some adults do. He tried to convince us that YMCA stood for 'Young Monkeys Cannot Act'. The YMCA was the social centre for the tiny Protestant community where young people could meet together and so avoid mixed marriages. Lay Roman Catholics generally did not understand that the reason for exclusive Protestant social life was the rule of the Catholic Church that required the children of mixed marriages to be brought up as Roman Catholics. The Protestant community guarded strongly this social exclusiveness in order to protect itself from the unjust rule that was decimating its already small numbers. One evening my sister was told by a member of the committee that Joan, a young Roman Catholic friend she had brought with her to the YMCA would have to leave.

In winter Mrs Scanlon scared us stiff with ghost stories. In summer we sat with her at the drawing room window overlooking the Bull Ring. This was before television, when not everybody had a wireless and when a summer evening's entertainment for some was to promenade on the Main Street. An evening's entertainment for us was to sit and watch them. Mrs Scanlon would comment humorously on anybody unusual that passed and she had her own nicknames for some of them. There were two regulars, women, one tall and thin and the other small and fat. The smaller one linked the arm of the taller one who carried a large handbag in the other hand at the end of a stiff, motionless arm. Despite a warm evening they both wore coats and hats and they never seemed to speak. My sister and I might be playing at something when Mrs Scanlon would call us: 'Here come Fatty Arbuckle and Skinny Liz.' She knew all the characters of the town. There was Tommy Swift, a man of stunted growth with a wrinkled face that didn't match his height but betrayed his age. He sold newspapers and wheeled a hand truck along the Main Street to the North Station to collect the Dublin papers from the train for Bucklands newsagents. Some of the wags of the town gave him a hard time and to us children he was a bad humoured little man. We had a joke:

'Tommy Swift is in hospital.'

'What's wrong with him?'

'Growing pains.'

There was Filthy Paddy the pig man. With an ass and cart with a barrel on the back he collected domestic slops to feed pigs. He wore a filthy dirty rain-coat that was in tatters and the cart and barrel were caked with dried slops. Unlike Tommy Swift he was good-humoured, smiled and he spoke to children. We had a rhyme about him:

> There's going to be a race
> Between two asses and a jennet,
> I'll bet you ten to one
> Filthy Paddy's ass'll win it.

There was Tommy Roche. He was a lay teacher in the Christian Brothers junior school opposite Dr Pierce's house on George's Street. I have no doubt he was 'Mr' to his face but he was 'Tommy' to everyone behind his back. He once said 'hello' to me on the street and in my innocence I said 'Hello Tommy' back to him, never having heard him called anything else. He suddenly became cross: 'What's your name?' I told him.

'I'll tell your mother. I'm Mr Roche.'

I told him I was sorry and he never did tell my mother, or if he did she never said. He was a stout man and walked with his hands behind his back and seemed all of the time to observe. He wasn't married, and in his later fifties he was ordained priest and became Fr Roche. I have no doubt the boys he taught still called him 'Tommy' behind his back.

Watching the world pass by with Mrs Scanlon was an entertaining way to spend a summer evening when going to bed in daylight made the telling of ghost stories pointless. She amused us too by doing card tricks. We thought she was magic, and she would never show us how to do them. It wasn't just a case of doing the tricks, she told long elaborate and absorbing stories to go with many of them.

If there were particularly good films in the Abbey Cinema and also in one of the other two of the town's cinemas, at around nine o'clock from the open window we could hear people passing in numbers on the footpath below. We could hear their voices and their footfall, but the balcony of the shop prevented us from seeing them. They made their way from the first house at the Abbey Cinema in George's Street down Cornmarket and along the Main Street to get the second house at the Cinema Palace or the Capitol at the other end of town. We could hear a similar rush going in the opposite direction within a few minutes. Cinema was one of the few affordable ways of escape for people of limited means in those days. Eileen, our maid, used to regale my mother with the stories of films and details about their heart-throbs, as though they were all in the real world.

When I was a child my mother always had a maid in the house. Some of them left to go to England and some of them didn't last long because they stole things and were fired. One of these, when challenged, finally confessed to stealing and in mitigation of her case informed my mother insolently that anyway it wasn't a sin to steal from a Protestant. She was in the tradition of the mediaeval Sienese merchants who when the Pope excommunicated their bankers felt no further obligation to repay their loans.

Eileen was the maid I remember best. Her mother had died and left a big family for Eileen's father to rear. He was a strict disciplinarian struggling to bring up the younger ones with the help of the older girls. He was not above taking his belt even to the girls when he considered it necessary, and I have no doubt that if Eileen had stolen anything he would have beaten her to within an inch of her life. He drove a jennet and cart for Godkin's bakery a few doors along the Main Street from where we lived. He was a small man, white from head to foot from carrying sacks of flour on his back. He wore a cap that was angled to the same degree as his back from the way he carried the sacks, bending forward, holding them at the top. On his return journey to the cart to carry another sack into the shop the cap, almost vertical, stayed miraculously in place. On a wet day he used a jute sack to cover his shoulders.

Eileen's father was delighted when she came to work for my mother – another wage, small though it was, to help with feeding and clothing the family. Eileen had to hand her whole wage to her father every Friday and he gave her back pocket money for the week. After she had been working for us for a few months she came to live-in and had a comfortable room to herself in the attic, rather than having to share a room with five or six siblings and share a bed with some of them. My mother taught her personal hygiene and how to look after herself and she gave her clothes and bought things for her that she needed.

Eileen was great fun and played with my sister and me when my mother wasn't around. Sometimes my mother got her to take us out for a walk and on one of these walks she called into Rowe Street Chapel where on entering the porch my sister took off through the door and up the church with Eileen in pursuit. The door swung closed leaving me in the dark porch not knowing what was going on as people came and went blessing themselves with water from the stoup, a strange ritual to an abandoned eight-year-old Protestant child. I was sure, that since I knew I shouldn't be there, somebody would take me by the ear and deposit me outside the gate. Eventually Eileen returned with my sister by the arm and marched her, followed by me, all the way home.

Occasionally if I was out with Eileen on my own she would call in to her home. It was a small terraced house in Duke's Lane off John Street opposite Rowe Street Chapel. It had no more than two or three rooms. There was a fire at the far end of the small downstairs room and one small window that let in limited light through a net curtain black with dirt. The room was dark and it took a while for my eyes to adjust. There was a bare wooden table under the window and three or four chairs and a dresser against the end wall. The room was airless and had an all-pervasive smell of poverty.

As soon as we arrived I was brought up to sit in an honoured place beside the open fire that was on the floor under a wide chimney. I was given a bit of bread and butter that I didn't want but knew it would be impolite not to take. One of Eileen's brothers or sisters would talk to me and ask me questions and before I left, to my embarrassment, one of them always insisted on giving me a penny. I tried to refuse it but they insisted. I always spent the penny on sweets that I shared with Eileen before I got home for I knew my parents would be cross with me for taking it. They wouldn't have understood how hard it was to refuse. I'm sure it was Eileen's family's way of showing their appreciation of my mother looking after her.

One Saturday my mother delegated Eileen to take us to the circus but when we got to the field the circus hadn't arrived and the performance was cancelled. We were deeply disappointed so to compensate us Eileen took it upon herself to buy us all large ice creams with the circus money. We, of course, were delighted, but I was sure that this unauthorised initiative would get her into trouble but to my surprise my mother never said a word.

Inevitably, with stories coming back across the Irish Sea of streets 'paved with gold', and with older brothers and a sister there, Eileen took the boat to England. My sister and I were getting older and my mother did not replace her. I missed her as I was fond of her and we got on well together. She was fun and she stood up for me with my sister and even with my parents from time to time.

My mother was a tea connoisseur and as any tea connoisseur will tell you, in order to make a decent pot of tea the quality of the water is as important as the quality of the tea. She considered the town supply unsuitable for this purpose, so one of Eileen's jobs had been to go for spring water that was kept specially for tea. Now that Eileen had gone my mother sent my sister or me to what was for us an unfamiliar part of town, to a public spout that carried the best of spring water. I knew that when I went there, as a strange boy on his own, I was vulnerable to questioning and possibly to attack by local boys. Gangs of boys in certain parts of town were territorial and you were at risk if you ventured onto their patch. On one occasion I was cornered by a group of boys who interrogated me. They asked my name, where I lived and where I went to school.

'Then you're a Protestant.'

'Yes.'

'Your priests get married.'

'Yes.' I said. To which there were knowing grins between them. Then they informed me in an unmistakably superior way that their priests and brothers didn't get married because they didn't do 'the dirty thing.'

Furthermore I didn't like going to the spring for water as it was an interruption to my own plans and I thought it was a strange thing to have to do since none of my friends had to collect water for making tea. Their mothers seemed content with water from the tap and one thing a young boy does not want to be is different from his friends. I knew that these reasons would cut no ice with my mother so I solved the problem when I discovered a tap just inside the gate of an open yard opposite Hanton's undertakers on John Street – a shorter journey from home and in an area where I was safe. I used to fill the can there and take my time coming and going and my mother never discovered my secret. In due course she stopped sending us for water, presumably because she believed the quality of water from the spring was no better than that from the tap.

A year or so after Eileen left I was playing one afternoon in the back yard when my mother called me: 'Eileen is here to see you.' I rushed up to the drawing room and in the door in great excitement. There she was. High heels, hair dyed, heavily made up and dressed to the nines. I stopped short. She spoke to me, and I knew there was something different. She had a strange accent. My heart sank. She said: 'Hello, Pat. My, you've grown.'

'Hello,' I said.

'Do you remember the fun we used to have?'

'Yes.' Then she spoke to my mother. I stayed for a little while and she spoke to me again. She wasn't the Eileen I remembered and after a minute or two I went back to the yard. I almost cried with disappointment that the person in the drawing room could be such a different person to my one time friend.

Living on the Main Street we were at the centre of things in a way we were not when we lived on Hill Street. Thursday was half day when shops on the Main Street closed at one o'clock. Sports were played on Thursday afternoons and Billy Malone took out his horse-drawn charabanc and went for a drive. Billy was a small stoutish man who ran a vegetable shop. He was bald on top, but grew his hair long on one side of his head and drew it across his bald pate to the other side and stuck it down with hair oil. In a high wind the streak of hair blew off and fluttered in the breeze revealing his baldness for all the world to see. In addition to vegetables he sold rabbits, which he skinned and hung in bunches of protruding eyes and shiny pink flesh outside the door of his shop.

Shopkeepers made up for Thursday afternoon's early closing when they stayed open on Saturday night until nine o'clock. Saturday was the day that country people came to town to shop and the Main Street was packed most of the day with pedestrians walking, not only on the footpaths but on the street. Country people, not used to footpaths and used only to occasional traffic seemed to resent having to move from the middle of the street. A cyclist or a motor car driver could travel at no more than a crawl for fear of hitting a pedestrian preoccupied with shop windows and bargains. A boy I knew whose father owned a garage yoked up a car battery and horn in the basket of his sister's bike one Saturday. He cycled quietly up behind some of these unsuspecting country people on the street and blew the horn causing consternation. The guards discovered him and put an end to his prank for fear he would cause somebody an untimely death by heart attack.

Connie Godfrey was a regular shopper in Wexford. In summer she ran a guesthouse, 'The Corral' on the Burrow road on the edge of the village of Kilmore Quay. It was her home; she would not have sought, and if she had she would not have received, Bórd Fáilte approval as she ran it her own way. During the season she was full, and the overflow of her guests, most of whom came back year after year, were happy to stay in makeshift accommodation, including an old caravan in the yard. They were literally guests in her home and dinner in the evening was the highlight of the day. Connie presided at the head of the table complete with family silver. Dinner, of three or maybe four courses, was a no nonsense meal of the highest quality, and was taken slowly over the best part of two hours, and served by Mickey.

Mickey had been a fiddler in the orchestra of the D'Oyly Carte Opera Company that came on a tour to Wexford. Connie's eye fell on him and he never went back. He was a cultured person, as was Connie, and they lived together in an indeterminate relationship in 'The Corral'. Connie was a larger-than-life figure in every sense. She was a large stout woman whose size and configuration made it difficult for her to walk. Mickey used to take her in the car from the front of the house, where she sat during the day, out on the road and in the end gate and around the back to her bedroom at night. Mickey was a spare diminutive man who, on Connie's instructions, did everything.

He was an able musician and played the harmonium in the local Church of Ireland church at Balloughton. On Sundays during the summer he encouraged guests to go to church and sit beside the harmonium to help with the singing. The instrument had seen better days and was not up to standard for a professional musician. During the sermon Mickey would have one of his 'choir' hold a torch while he disassembled part of the harmonium and, with a screwdriver and pliers, root in the interior of the instrument in an effort to improve the sound or to stop a squeak. Whether he had an arrangement with the rector not to finish his sermon until the repairs were completed, or Mickey kept an ear on him and could predict when the rector was coming to an end, nobody knew. He never seemed to be caught unprepared for the hymn that followed the sermon. In the days when Connie was mobile enough to attend church she sat in the 'choir' with her two dogs on her lap and fed them sweets during the service.

On Saturdays Mickey drove Connie to Wexford to do the shopping. He drove along the Main Street and stopped at the door of the shops where she dealt. Connie, who would have found it impossible to get in and out of the car, called from the passenger seat and the shopkeeper would come out and take her order. They all knew her well. Later Mickey would drive her on a second circuit of the Main Street, when a beep of the horn was a signal to the shopkeeper to bring her shopping out to the car.

Saturday was also the day for the afternoon matinee in the cinemas. The films were for children, and most often cowboy ones when the 'goodie' despite the odds being against him, always came out on top. In our house Saturday was the day for the administration of senna tea. A miscalculation of its strength sometimes meant a desperate dash for home from the cinema before the end, thereby missing the serial, designed to attract you back the following week, or even missing the end of the main film and the triumph of good over evil.

By contrast with Saturday, on Sundays the Main Street was deserted. Every shop was bolted and barred and if there was an important GAA match involving Wexford broadcast on Radio Éireann, Fran Leary the cobbler who lived just off the Bull Ring in Cornmarket opened his door and played Michael O'Hehir's commentary of the match at full volume. It blared out desecrating the Sunday afternoon and I have no doubt it could be heard at the far end of the town. Nobody ever seemed to stand to listen to it, but this did not deter Fran from his public-spirited act to enable those who had no wireless to hear the match. We lived three doors away from this monstrous intrusion into the peace and quiet of a Sunday afternoon and for my parents it was, to say the least, incompatible with the observance of a Protestant Sunday.

2

Childhood

Much of the activity of the Christian Church is about the exercise of power and control over their members in order to ensure the well-being or even the survival of the ecclesiastical institution. Nowhere is this more evident than in the area of education. In the south of Ireland the Churches see control of schools, especially at primary level, as fundamental to their well-being. This of course is true in other countries too, but in Ireland control of denominational schools, at present part of the state education system, will be the last and fiercest battle to be fought between Church and State. The Churches will join forces for this battle, in fact they already line up together on issues against the Department of Education. They see denominational education as the very bedrock of their control and upon which their well-being or even their survival depends. Continuing Church membership is perceived to depend on early education or indoctrination and, with the benefits of psychological insights, it is with good reason the Churches believe this.

It is possible that children of different religions could be educated in the same schools and be separated only for religious education. This is beginning to happen in the 'Educate Together' movement and in some of the Gaelscoileanna. This kind of arrangement, however, is not acceptable to the Churches on the principle that religion is caught not taught. It is communicated as much, if not more, through our emotions and our senses as through our minds. Each Church wants control of their own schools as much to create their own religious ethos as to teach their own doctrine. This mysterious abstract quality 'ethos' that Churches talk about but don't define is a bit like a headache in that you know when it is present or absent but you have great difficulty in saying what it is. A recent education act uses the term 'characteristic spirit.'

In the 1940s and 1950s denominational control of schools was absolute. The state paid teachers and grant-aided schools that were run by the different Churches. Each primary school was run by what was known as the 'single clerical manager', who was the local parish priest, Church of Ireland rector or Nonconformist minister. With only the rarest of exceptions Roman Catholics went to Catholic managed schools and Protestants went to Protestant managed schools and during the period of the curriculum allowed for religious education they were indoctrinated in the religion to which they belonged by teachers of their own religion. It was virtually unknown for a teacher to teach in a school of a religion other than their own, and they were expected to promote religion as part of their duties. They were expected to actively promote the relationship between the school and the Church. An atheist or agnostic teacher in Ireland in those days, though a rare bird, was unemployable. Secondary schools were also under the control of the Churches.

When I was a child in Wexford there was still one private school run by an individual teacher in her home, Miss Price on Jail Road, which was not under Church control. It was definitely Protestant and in the tradition of private schools of earlier times. So good was the state primary system and of course free, that Miss Price closed her school for lack of numbers. When it closed the few remaining children, no more than a half dozen, came to the Church of Ireland National School.

In the nineteenth century and up to this time these small private schools provided education for families that could pay fees and no doubt there was kudos or snobbery attached to education in a private rather than a state school. At the end of the nineteenth century and earlier in the twentieth there had been a number of such schools in Wexford to which the children of business and professional Protestant families sent their children. A Miss Shaw ran one over a little shop in Selskar with an assistant Miss May Hornick, and Miss Furney ran a school in George's Street. Miss

Ethel Rowe, who came home to look after her parents when they were old, opened a little school in Richmond Terrace on Spawell Road. Running private schools appears to have been an occupation for maiden ladies, and while I know Miss Rowe was one of Ireland's early women graduates, I don't know if the others had academic qualifications or not.

From the late 1940s No 4 National School in St Patrick's Square with its one teacher, Miss Mary Sherwood, was the only Protestant primary school in Wexford. The Sherwoods came to Wexford when Mary's father, a member of the RIC, was transferred there. She and her siblings had been to school at Patrick's Square with my father and his siblings. Now the school catered for all the Protestant children of the town and of the surrounding countryside. Canon Hazley was the manager and he was responsible for the administration of the school and for the arrangements to bring the country children in every day by hackney car. He was also responsible for maintaining the connection between the school and the parish. The school had to maintain a certain number of pupils, as a one teacher school, to remain viable. If the numbers fell below this figure there was a danger the Department of Education would withdraw their support, so keeping up numbers was a constant problem. The situation was helped by the arrival of English families, the fathers of which came to work in Wexford.

In the late 1940s and early 1950s the three main industries were Pierce's Foundry, well known to farmers throughout the country and abroad for their agricultural implements and machinery, the Star Iron Works that also manufactured farm implements and Hadden's furniture factory. After the war Englishmen with technical skills came to work in all these businesses.

Pierce's had built an avenue of houses called Avenue de Flandres near the foundry in which they housed the families of some of the men who came from England to work for them. There were six houses and families from England or Wales occupied three of them: the Owens, Pavers and McQuillans who lived in a row and in the other three there were Irish families. Collins, a superintendent of the gardaí, Glynn, a bank official at the Munster and Leinster Bank on North Main Street and Drurys one of whom worked in the County Library. Two Englishmen, Wheeler and Howlin, came to work in Hadden's factory and another, Hume, came to the Star. Some of these people from the UK were Nonconformist and went to the Presbyterian Church, most were Anglican and were distinguished by their non-attendance at the Church of Ireland Church. I never saw any of the husbands in Church and the wives only rarely, and then usually when they had children and there was a service connected with the school. Those families that had children helped to keep up the school numbers but they were no addition to the parish.

Despite what I believe many Roman Catholics might have thought, the Englishness of these families marked them off from the Irishness of the indigenous Protestant families. Though of the same religion the adults shared little in common. At the prompting of the rector my parents were glad to invite one of these men, who had arrived in Wexford alone ahead of his wife and daughter, to Sunday lunch. After lunch the conversation turned to the issue of nationality, and perhaps conscious of being different, the visitor refused to acknowledge English/Irish differences. He harped on for some time and wouldn't let go. He eventually asked my father: 'If you weren't Irish what would you like to be?'

By this time he had irritated my father beyond endurance who replied: 'Dead', and put an abrupt end to that particular topic.

The children of these English families were different too. They were in some ways more advanced, or perhaps the word is precocious. One of the girls caused consternation when she took it upon herself to inform her Irish school friend, to the child's utter incredulity, about the facts of life, something that in those days was not mentioned at home, let alone on the school curriculum. But at the end of the day, children being children, we got on well together and I spent many a day playing in the fields around Avenue de Flandres with Richard Paver and the Collins and Glynn children.

Amongst us children religion or nationality did not enter into it at all, or almost not at all. One night Stan, the youngest of the Glynn boys stayed the night with Richard Paver and to Stan's mother's amazement he wet the bed, which he hadn't done since he was a small boy. Mrs Glynn, having questioned him couldn't fathom it and eventually asked him if he had gone to the bathroom before he went to bed.

'No,' he replied.

'Why not?'

'Because I wouldn't pee in a Protestant lavatory!'

Learning Irish was the thing the English children found most difficult in school. This was mitigated somewhat by Miss Sherwood being a lover of and an enthusiast for the language. She used it on every conceivable occasion and taught it well. So much so that later on one English boy she had started on Irish became fluent and was chairman of the Irish Society at university. Many indigenous Protestant children also found Irish difficult, which wasn't helped by the negative attitude of the parents of some children who saw the compulsory teaching of the language as a manifestation of aggressive nationalism with which they were not in sympathy. Others who understood education as no more than a means of getting a job, or a time to be endured before returning to the farm, held the view that Irish was of no practical use. My parents were not at all unsympathetic to Irish but had none themselves. When he heard my sister or me learning Irish poetry or spellings my father would make his own contribution with the following gibberish: 'Cum a heck pie chu clay alice copaken leekin and dread bore a hole in a mahogany gaspipe okey dokey swallidy ponk.'

Almost all the English families sent their children to local Catholic schools for their secondary education while the indigenous Protestant families sent their children away to Protestant boarding schools. Of the families that came from England during my time, all returned. None settled permanently in Wexford.

When I was about ten I was sent to Miss Price after school hours to learn piano. The simple fact of the matter was that I had no talent for or interest in it and bad and all as it was to have to go to lessons, having to practise was worse. After some time my mother came to the conclusion that I wasn't making much progress and I was sent for lessons to Miss Mary Codd, a noted musician and the organist in both Rowe Street and Bride Street Catholic churches. There didn't seem to be a problem with 'ethos' in the learning of music.

Miss Codd lived on the Main Street opposite Woolworths, in a house with a black door and a big brass knocker. She lived on the first floor and her piano was along the wall behind the door in the sitting room straight ahead at the top of the stairs, overlooking the Main Street. She kept the blinds one-third of the way down and in the two window recesses on tall stands there were brass pots containing maidenhair fern that fell to the floor. There were full-length net curtains in swags on either side of the recesses that removed the possibility of seeing anything of the outside world. On the end wall stood an elaborately ornate glass case full of china, glass and knick-knacks. The furniture was undisturbed from week to week. There was no strong colour in the room and the whole atmosphere was dismal. It was clear that the piano and piano stool were the only items in the room that were used.

Miss Codd conducted the lesson in a rather more directive way than Miss Price had done. She held a pointer to the music and used it to direct my hands when they were in the wrong place, as they often were. When I performed particularly badly she tapped my knuckles to the accompaniment of her verbal admonition. The carrot she held out to me, as she insisted on the importance of exercises and scales, was to be able to play 'Tweedle Dum and Tweedle Dee' with both hands!

One day after school I arrived for a music lesson and knocked the big brass knocker. No reply. I knocked again. Still no reply, so I went home, pleased with myself, to inform my mother that Miss Codd was not there. It transpired that she had forgotten the lesson, which my mother perfectly understood. I had however taken note, and a few weeks later, when I knew I was ill prepared for the lesson I arrived at the door and knocked gently on the big brass knocker. No reply. I knocked again even more gently, and still no reply. I went home pleased with myself again to inform my mother that Miss Codd wasn't there. When approached she insisted that she was there, but my ruse had thrown doubt in my mother's mind on Miss Codd's reliability. I insisted that she wasn't there. After all hadn't I knocked twice but maybe, I suggested, she was in the bathroom and couldn't answer the door.

As it happened the summer holidays and my departure for boarding school forestalled the controversy. This development did nothing for my commitment to learn music, indeed it diminished it considerably as piano lessons competed with sport and as far as I was concerned there was no contest. Furthermore, the music teacher at The King's Hospital, Mr O'Callaghan, who came into school only to teach piano, was neurotic. He had thick black hair on the backs of his hands and he smiled sweetly when you arrived for your lesson. He stood well back from the piano and if he detected that you had the hint of a cold he stood back at the door. If you gave the appearance of being entirely healthy and he found it necessary to demonstrate by playing a portion of music himself he first wiped the keyboard with his handkerchief and asked you to stand back while he demonstrated. He also wiped the handle of the door before turning it. He marked each lesson out of five and I never got more than three. Eventually my parents realised they were fighting a losing battle and allowed me to abandon the piano. When I was younger an old gentleman we called Pa Price came to our house for the evening every Saturday night. When I began to learn music he told me sagely never to give up the piano, that if I did I would always regret it. He was right.

Playing indoors is for winter, playing outside and venturing abroad is for summer. Being brought up beside the sea I could swim from an early age. I don't remember learning. During the long school summer holidays we rolled our togs in a towel, put it on the carrier of the bike and cycled to the 'Bathing Place' near the hundred year old or more New Bridge, leading to Ferrybank, or to Curracloe seven miles away. In good weather we swam at least twice a day. We sometimes went to Ferrybank on the ferry that ran across the river roughly where the present bridge is. A man called Doherty who sold newspapers owned the boat, an ordinary large rowing boat, and by two o'clock on a fine summer day there was a queue of mothers and grandmothers with a hundred shouting and excited children on the short pier waiting to cross. Mr Doherty employed a man to do the rowing, and at sixpence for adults and three pence for children he packed the boat and headed off into the river to ease down with the tide onto the beach at Ferrybank. Depending on the state of the tide the rowing might be easy or it might be tough. Early afternoon he returned empty for another load and by mid-afternoon the traffic was in the opposite direction. There were no such things as lifebelts for passengers or crew and on warm sunny days the boat was usually overloaded. Nobody, owner or parents, seemed to be aware of the danger, but while I was a child there was never an accident. We were able to dive at full tide at the 'Bathing Place' or off the back of the pier at Ferrybank, where it was considered dangerous to swim at all.

When we were a little older we joined the boat club to play tennis. We were weekday junior members and could play during the day when most adult members were at work. Nobody trained us but we belted the ball about after the fashion of the proper game and when we were tired of that we went into the boathouse in the hope some senior member might be about to take out a boat. Sometimes we would volunteer to row a senior member up the river simply to get out on the water. We weren't allowed to go alone. The days were long and fine and warm and we hadn't a care in the world.

A little older still, came cricket. The pitch was at Park and George Saville, whose father had come to Wexford to manage the gas works, ran the club. George's sister was married to one of my father's brothers. George worked for the gas company too, but in summer cricket took precedence over everything else in his life. The club was a one-man show; he mowed the pitch and marked the wicket, he kept the gear in order. He rounded up enough people to make up a team for a match, often fielding a side one or even two short or with schoolboys like myself as tail-enders. There were some good cricketers up the order and it happened from time to time that someone who had never played the game before filled one of the last places. The first question George asked an adult neophyte was: 'Are you a hurler? Well like hurling keep your eye on the ball and keep it out of your wicket.' Cricket was a quintessentially middle-class game and the club was about fifty/fifty Catholic/Protestant, most of whom had learned their cricket at school.

There were cricket teams in most of the surrounding provincial towns: Enniscorthy, Carlow, Bagenalstown, Waterford. We played estate teams, Coolattin and Mount Juliet, and there were teams in small County Wexford villages like Broadway and Tacumshane. The town and estate teams had good pitches, reasonable players and observed the customs and traditions of the game, whereas the village teams paid them scant attention. Games were played on half-day Thursday and Sunday afternoons. The team assembled at White's Hotel at one o'clock for away matches and those with cars collected those without. During summer holidays my cousin Michael, George's nephew, was over from London staying with the Savilles. Michael and I travelled with George and his long time girlfriend Patsy in his soft-top MG TD. This made for a speedy and exhilarating journey with the top down on a warm summer day. George and Patsy couldn't marry because he was Protestant, though he never appeared in church, and she was Catholic. Years later when his father retired George left Ireland and went with the family to England. Early in the cricket season, before Michael arrived in Wexford for the summer, when I was on my own at Whites waiting for a lift, I was invariably allocated to Mr Le Blanc. He was a bachelor schoolmaster accompanied by his maiden aunt Miss Roberts, who used to run the Eason's stand on the North Station. Bill Le Blanc drove a Ford Popular!

Playing one of the village sides you discovered the pitch was nowhere near the village and the thing you noticed on a first visit was that there was no pavilion. The visitors changed at the boot of their cars on the side of a narrow country road. The field, that had sheep, if not cattle, on it up to a few days before the match had recently been cut and the wicket, though slightly better than the outfield, was a trifle agricultural. Most of the home team didn't wear whites. Some of them wore white shirts with their Sunday suit trousers and braces and some of them wore tennis shoes. Others arrived dressed as they were and simply took off their jackets. The home team more than likely had only two pairs of usable pads. They either borrowed a pair from the visitors, or the incoming batsman had to wait until the wicket fell and pad up half way to the crease with the pads from the batsman on his way out, and possibly use his bat too.

A visitor would make a bad mistake if he thought that all of this meant the match would be a pushover. These cute country-men might not have observed the customs, but they had a firm grasp of the essentials of the game and local conditions were to their advantage. Visiting batsmen had to revise their assumptions about the behaviour of the ball off the wicket and an underarm throw-in from the boundary, after the manner of County Cork 'bowlers,' would arrive through the air at the wicket-keeper with deadly speed and accuracy. The conditions of the outfield made anything other than singles or sixes hard to achieve and this, the enthusiasm of the fielders and the fact they were used to their own sub-standard wicket, made the home side hard to beat.

In contrast to all of this a game at Coolattin was idyllic. The match was played on a perfectly kept wicket on a ground in the middle of the estate, surrounded by mature trees emitting a variety of birdsong, to the constant background sound of a swiftly flowing river nearby. There was a Victorian pavilion with verandah and all the traditions and customs of the game were observed. The sound of ball on bat and the occasional ripple of applause from the pavilion seemed almost a violation of the tranquillity of the place, to say nothing of the over enthusiastic appeals of a bowler or wicket-keeper.

The match with Fishguard was an important annual fixture. Either they crossed the Irish Sea on the Rosslare ferry to us or we went in the opposite direction to play them. This fixture created an interesting situation for Ted Dougall, the radio officer on one of the ferries, who when he was in port in Fishguard played for them and when in Rosslare played for Wexford. When playing this international fixture between the two clubs, however, his first loyalty was Fishguard.

Once a year the Leprechauns came to Wexford for an all-day game bringing some notable names from Dublin and national cricket. The Leprechauns were a team, rather than a club. They had no premises or pitch and the team consisted of members of established clubs who joined by invitation. They played only at intervals throughout the season, either to support the promotion of cricket or to play special or festival games. The social dimension to a Leprechauns' visit was one of the highlights of the season for Wexford Cricket Club. It was an all-day game and the teams withdrew to White's Hotel for what usually became an extended, and for some a liquid, lunch. On returning to the pitch, one or two of the players found their ability to time the ball, or even to see it properly, somewhat impaired after a particularly relaxed lunch.

It was an opportunity for local enthusiasts to see such well-known names of the Irish cricketing world as Louis Jacobson, Paddy Boland and many others, play. The strength of the visitors compared to the home side meant the game was often over earlier than usual which led to extended time available for sociability after it, before the Leprechauns returned to Dublin.

For holidays during the war we went to a farm guesthouse outside Aughrim, Co Wicklow, which meant other families with children, warm summer days, collecting eggs, milking cows and trying the patience of men at work. We would wander through fields afraid and not afraid of cattle, but well-versed as to how to tell if there was a bull, frightening each other that there was. Or into the forest to watch men fell and take out trees with horse and tackle and play on piles of conifer logs, hands and clothes covered in resin for parents to remove with butter. All hands to help at haymaking; tea and sandwiches in the field and sitting on top of the load of hay in the shed, jumping, tumbling and falling after the men had gone for another load. My memories of holidays: the smell of resin, hay and rashers frying. Brown bread, country butter and raspberry jam, all homemade. Keeping going till bedtime, tired from country air and exercise, sleep and more tomorrow.

After the war holidays were a cottage in Rosslare. Sea, sand and swimming; in bare feet all day. A hideout below deck in an old, beached boat where older ones smoke, one a pipe, and suffocate the rest. Tennis and riding horses from a local stable through dunes and along the beach. Wandering on the strand edge of the golf links and finding lost balls. Like Aughrim, freedom and non-stop until late bedtime, tired from sea air, sleep and more tomorrow.

One post-war holiday was to England to the Sussex coast. We crossed Rosslare to Fishguard overnight and slept in a bunkroom in the suffocating bowels of the ferry. The endless train journey Fishguard to London, and a day with cousins to see the sights: Trafalgar Square, Buckingham Palace and Madame Tussaud's. A train to St Leonards for a more civilised seaside holiday than Rosslare; a supervised beach with deckchairs, bathing booths and a flag to tell you when to swim or not to swim. One night a firework display after dark with candyfloss, lemonade and a late, late bedtime and more sophisticated holiday things to do tomorrow.

Christmas in our house was quiet. My mother's brother, Tom, sometimes came home from London where he was a civil servant in the Ministry of Supply. He had played rugby for London Irish and one year he and another London Irish player were selected for an Irish trial. They travelled by train and boat arriving in Dublin in the early morning of the match after a rough crossing. Tom's excuse for neither of them having been selected was that not only were they suffering from lack of sleep, but as a result of the sedative effect of an overdose of anti-seasick pills, neither of them was fully awake until half way through the second half.

While Uncle Tom was with us for Christmas he used to sit and read and go for long walks. I sometimes set out on these walks with him but I couldn't keep up and turned around and came home. One year while he was sitting reading he offered me half a crown on the condition that I didn't sing 'Rudolph the Red-Nosed Reindeer' again until after he had gone back. I took the bribe, but had to be reminded a few times not to break the contract.

Tom had been a civil servant in Dublin before the formation of the State and in 1922 opted to go to London. This was not a political decision. At the time he was, as they used to say in those days, 'walking out' with Julia, also a civil servant. She was Roman Catholic and her family would not have accepted her marriage to a Protestant. Tom's family, apart from my mother, wouldn't have been over the moon about it either. So they both opted to go to London and did the next best thing; they lived together. This may also have been because if they had married she would have had to leave her job in the civil service. At Christmas Julia went home to her family in the midlands, who knew nothing of Tom, and he either came to us or went to a brother in Cork.

After Tom died Julia and my mother stayed in touch, and when Julia retired she came back to live in Ireland. In my late teens, some eight years after Tom's death, I had occasion to visit the town where Julia lived and my mother told me to call and see her. I did and she was delighted to see me. She talked movingly about Tom and with tears in her eyes she said: 'And I haven't even got his name.' Before I left she said, 'I have something for you; I've been keeping them.' She left the room and came back with Tom's watch and his golf clubs.

When I was a child I had friends that were both Catholic and Protestant. They were in and out of my home and I was in and out of theirs. Religion wasn't an issue for me or for my family. Naturally as I grew up I began to notice differences. Sunday for me was observed with my family. I didn't normally play with friends of either tradition. We stayed indoors or went for a walk. Later on, however, cricket was deemed to be sufficiently sedate not to violate the Sabbath. I had a sense that for some reason the criterion for Sunday observance was not to be out in public where there were large numbers of people. To go to the pictures was out of the question. I remember the guilt I felt later on when I lived in Dublin and went to the pictures on Sunday for the first time.

Of course Catholics making the sign of the cross, which seemed to be done more frequently then than it is today, reminded me of the difference, and the fact that Catholics would say 'Thank God,' while Protestants were more likely to say 'Thank goodness.' I remember only a couple of occasions being starkly reminded that I was a Protestant. Once was with some Catholic friends who were talking about their plans to join the scouts. One of them turned to me and said simply and matter-of-factly: 'Oh you can't, you're a Protestant.'

3

Boarding School

For secondary education my parents decided I would go as a boarder to The King's Hospital in Dublin. In order to gain admission I had to pass the entrance exam, so in June of 1951 I went with my mother by train to Dublin to sit the exam. Miss Sherwood, my teacher, and my parents spoke of it as a matter of great seriousness as though my whole life depended upon it. The apparent importance of it did not impinge on me; I considered it an inconvenience. The only compensation was two days off school and a trip to Dublin.

I had been in Dublin once before, when I was eight. It was a Sunday and the only time I remember as a child missing church. Dorothy, a niece of my father, who had been staying on holiday with us was going back to England and she had to catch a flight from Collinstown in the early afternoon. We left Wexford by hackney car at about 9 am and it seemed that in every town or village we drove through, people were coming out of Mass and walking across the street in front of the car causing us to slow down. I remember Arklow in particular where the Mass-goers poured across the street like milk poured from a pail, as though recently acquired grace had made them immune from the danger of oncoming traffic. We had to stop until they cleared. It appeared that the virtue of having been at Mass gave them precedence over motor traffic on the road. We drove through Dublin to the airport, saw Dorothy off and drove straight back to Wexford. As there were no evening Masses in those days, I don't remember, but I assume we had a clear run.

My mother and I arrived at Westland Row station on the afternoon before the entrance exam and went by horse cab to the Central

Hotel on the corner of Exchequer Street and Georges Street. An early night was prescribed, but Exchequer Street, Dublin was not the Bull Ring, Wexford. The intention of an early night was frustrated by the noise of the city and especially the squealing brakes of the buses that pulled in to a stop nearby. I woke many times before finally going to sleep when the traffic died down.

Next morning, wakened early by the sounds of the city, we had breakfast in the busy hotel dining room and crossed the river to Blackhall Place to The King's Hospital, formerly a charity school, but now an integral and respected part of the Irish Protestant education system. The atmosphere of the historic building was formidable as was the headmaster the Rev J.J. Butler, a big man with a dark suit, clerical collar and a sonorous voice of unmistakable authority. He marshalled the examinees to a classroom at the end of a long stone-flagged passage, with desks laid out with boards and blotters in place for the exam. Already there was a begowned, bald master in the room, with a round face, to whom the headmaster spoke, before calling a roll using surnames only, and then disappearing. The master distributed the question paper, silence descended and we set into arithmetic. Almost immediately clicked fingers attracted the master's attention and disturbed the rest of us. With a serious face, just short of a frown of disapproval at the click, he looked at the paper and listened to the query. Then without a word, a smile transformed the master's face that said to the boy, 'that's for you to find out'.

There was a break, another paper and then the head prefect, who looked too old to be still at school, brought us to lunch. The large rectangular dining hall at the other end of the school had a strong smell of floor polish. We filled one of the long tables. Half way through our lunch the whole school filed into the dining hall in line and filled the other tables. After a Latin grace we finished our meal to the deafening chatter of more than a hundred boys free from morning class. The prefect brought us to the pitch outside to play for a short while with a cricket bat and ball before returning for a final paper. My mother collected me and we made for the evening train home.

I had had no sense of competing against the examiner or against the other examinees. I didn't think about doing well and I had no idea what would happen if I failed, but that never occurred to me either. I simply got on and did what I had to do. In due course my parents got word that I had passed the exam and I was on course to enter the school in the autumn.

On 10 September 1951 I entered The King's Hospital. My parents accompanied me to the school and the first person we met when we arrived was the Reverend R.H. Johnston, who had been for a short time acting headmaster of Tate School in Wexford. He spoke to the parents and ignored the boy. In response to my father's enquiry as to how much pocket money they should give me, he recommended £1 for the term. I never forgave him. It was never enough, but I would not have asked my parents for more. Other boys had twice and three times that. If there were those with less they never came to my notice.

My parents left me in the hands of a senior boy to help with my case, and then I explored the passages and found the big schoolroom. There were new boys like myself wandering about looking as lost as I was, some of whom I recognised from the entrance exam. I had an overwhelming feeling, not of loneliness or of having been abandoned but of wanting to know the right thing to do. The schoolroom slowly filled up with the noise and chatter of boys of every age and shape; new boys not knowing what was coming next and older ones relaxed and confident, some greeting each other as long lost brothers after the long summer holiday. I watched and waited.

Outside a bell was rung, the first of those that would govern every school day for the next four years. A prefect came up the centre passage of the schoolroom shouting at everybody to sit down, and slowly he brought about order from chaos. The entire school was seated by class, or almost the entire school, as a couple of latecomers arrived just in time before the head arrived. The room fell silent as he mounted the platform and leaned on the high desk while the head prefect below him called the roll - Boothman, Corrie, Ward, Rae, Dunne, Hunt … When he got to the new boys at the end some still answered 'anseo', the answer from their national schools, instead of the sophisticated 'adsum', one of the remnants of what had once been a classical education.

Then the whole school filed down in roll-order to the dining hall for tea. After grace, *Benedict, Domine, nos et haec tua dona, quae a bonatate tua, sumturi sumus,* we had bread, a pat of butter and, from an urn at the end of the table, tea with milk already added. Later we discovered that the tea was infused through a nylon bag that looked for all the world like a nylon stocking, and may well have been. There was Latin grace at the end of the meal that sounded to me like: '*Benedicto benedicatur, per Jesum Christum, Dan MacMaster*', and for ages I wondered who Dan MacMaster was! It was *Dominum Nostrum.* After tea we had time to ourselves followed by another bell that signalled bed.

'Fours', the junior dormitory, had approximately forty beds. Apart from beds the only piece of furniture in the room was a long cupboard in which in due course we hung our Sunday suits. Beside each bed there was a hook on the wall on which to hang a towel. The sheets and blankets were individually folded and placed in a pile on the pillow and the mattress was turned up to the head of the bed and rested on top of them. We had to leave our beds this way every morning and the boy guilty of sloppy work or of short-cuts in the performance of this duty was easily identified by the nametape on the towel hanging beside the offending bed and was punished accordingly. Every night each boy turned down the mat-tress and made his own bed. At some stage during this procedure the prefect responsible for the dormitory would dim the lights and shout 'prayers'. Each one knelt beside his bed to say his prayers, and should a boy not have many prayers to say and rise too soon, the prefect was likely to shout 'not enough' and the boy would have to kneel and address the Almighty again.

Every morning the bell woke us at 7.25 am when we trooped, half-asleep, down the stairs through a long passage and up more stairs to the stone-floored washroom to wash in cold water. We re-turned, dressed, made our beds and went to the big schoolroom for roll call at eight o'clock. The round of the day and the cycle of the weeks soon became familiar and life settled into a routine. Male teachers in gowns teaching different subjects in contrast to Mary in her twinset teaching everything. This was almost exclusively a male world; the only women in evidence were the matron and the kitchen maids.

It was also, with the exception of the groundsmen and kitchen staff, an all-Protestant world. In fact, in theory, it was exclusively Church of Ireland. There was a fine chapel with an Evie Hone window, into which we filed every weekday morning before class for a short service conducted by the Head and on Sundays for a full morning service. Despite the differences in religion I noted among my friends at home, I had no sense of the distinctive claims of different religions. I had recently become aware of the Roman Catholic Church's claim to be 'the one true Church', thereby, in the eyes of Roman Catholics, making the Church to which I belonged defective and incapable of delivering salvation. I did not know at this stage that there were some Protestants, even some evangelical members of the Church of Ireland, who believed that the Roman Catholic Church held so many false doctrines that Roman Catholics were automatically excluded from salvation and destined for hell.

Religion as I was taught it was about how you lived in this world and not how you got into the next one. I simply accepted religious differences as a fact of life without them having any particular significance for me. Apart from chapel services that became routine and religious education classes that were taught like any other subject, there wasn't a strong religious atmosphere in the school. Religion was, however, there in the background. In fact at this stage of my life I found sport more attractive than either schoolwork or religion.

I adapted without difficulty to boarding school life and went home contented for half term. I travelled by arrangement with Dyer and Ward, two senior boys. Shortly after the train started Dyer went to the bar and arrived back with two bottles of stout and a glass of lemonade for me. Ward, whose father knew my parents, occasionally essayed a conversation but conscious of their seniority I hadn't much to say to them. Dyer got off in Enniscorthy and Ward, who was going on to Rosslare, when we got to Wexford, opened the door and helped me down onto the platform to meet my mother. I could see it coming! As she approached, with my back to the carriage I shouted in a whisper: 'Don't kiss me, don't kiss me.'

During my time at home, mainly in reply to their questions, I gave my parents a bigger picture of my new life than I had done in my brief letters home. The first Wexford Festival was in full swing and my mother, intent on bringing me to something cultural, brought me to an art exhibition in the local 'tech'. On Sunday morning the family went to church as usual. After the service had started a tall, spare gentleman, wearing a tweed suit, sat into the pew in front of us. During the sermon he made notes on a piece of paper. When we stood for the hymn after the sermon I could see the piece of paper on the seat beside him. I had done enough Latin in half a term in school to know that he had made his notes in Latin, but I hadn't done enough to know what they said. The stranger was Lennox Robinson.

At the end of the half-term break I returned quite happily to school and then, from nowhere, bang, it hit me. On the first morning back in school I was crippled by an all-consuming bout of homesickness. I had noticed a few other boys suffering from it early in the term, but I didn't understand it. I didn't understand it now, but it devastated me. It is said that some people suffering from seasickness want to die. Since the only immediate way to get rid of homesickness, to go home, was out of the question I would happily have died. I cried myself to sleep at night and woke in the morning to the intense feeling of abandonment and isolation from parents and home which, since I felt it was unmanly and weak, I wouldn't reveal to anybody. I comported myself as normally as I could. My mind was taken off it to some extent by work in class, but when class was over I withdrew to one of the lavatory cubicles and cried my eyes out and emerged exhausted. I wrote home and told my parents about it and in reply I received words of comfort, which in fact made things worse, but there was no action. I prayed

fervently and frequently to God to take it away and received neither comfort nor action from Him. It went on unabated for three
or four days, then it slowly diminished and finally it was gone.
Only those who have endured homesickness will understand. I
never suffered from it again.

Before I went to boarding school I was already smoking the
odd Woodbine cigarette that some shopkeepers would sell singly
from the three-penny paper packet of five. In my first or second
year in school I smoked in school holidays but not in school. It
was safe to smoke on the way back in the train after the inspector
had checked my ticket. This opportunity, however, was frustrated
when Bill Le Blanc, bachelor schoolmaster, was returning in his
Ford Popular to Mountjoy School on the same day I was returning to KH. On these occasions he always offered to take me, and I
hated the three-hour journey. Shades of away cricket matches but
without the maiden aunt. After a few pleasantries I had nothing
to say to him and he had nothing to say to me, and the fact that
he smoked on the journey added frustration to my boredom. He
dropped me to the very door of the school making it impossible
either to buy cigarettes or to smoke them.

In third form I frequented the bicycle shed where the 'Smokers
Union' indulged its nefarious pursuit. One day the groundsman,
Eddie, told us he had been instructed by the Head to clean up
all the butts and matches that lay around; the inevitable detritus
of the Union's activities. A couple of days later, one by one, the
smokers were called out of second prep to be confronted by the
Headmaster on the matter of smoking and to be gated for the rest
of the term. Since I went out only on occasional exeats this wasn't
as severe a punishment for me as it was for boys who lived within
reach and went home every Sunday.

J.J. Butler ruled by fear and when he lost his temper, which
he did from time to time, he could be brutal. He was like most
religious authority figures in those days, in that when in control of
other people's children they had scant regard for the loving, caring,
forgiving teachings of the Gospel. They behaved as though they
were exempt from the teaching of the New Testament, and no

doubt if challenged they would quote Solomon's words: 'Spare the rod and spoil the child', from the Old Testament. Some of these people seemed to believe that to turn children into good Christians you sometimes had to literally beat the hell out of them. The excuse made today for these people is that they were different times, and these were people of their time. It must have been a time when the Church suspended the teachings of Jesus Christ and allowed brutal adults, especially religious ones, free rein.

Sport, and especially rugby, had a particular place in the life of the school. So much was this the case that in my first year the rugby captain of the First XV, Paul, though not a prefect, had the same power as prefects to give impositions. He did not, however, have a prefect's power to lurry, that is, to beat with the leather slipper. He was responsible for keeping rugby balls in good condition and if he saw a boy kicking a ball against a wall on the way back to the pavilion he would give the imposition to be written fifty or a hundred times, 'I must not kick Paul's balls against the walls.'

Apart from cup matches at the end of the season, rugby matches tended to be with other Protestant schools. I don't believe this was for sectarian reasons but because Protestant schools having smaller numbers to choose from generally played a lesser standard of rugby than Catholic schools that had much greater numbers from which to select teams. There were 140 pupils in KH when I went there in 1951. Some of the larger Catholic schools had twice this number or even more. In the cup competition towards the end of the season, if we advanced well in the early stages we usually ended up being beaten by Blackrock, Belvedere, Castleknock or Terenure. The 1950/1951 season was an exception when the senior team beat Catholic University Schools, Castleknock and Terenure, only to be beaten in the final by Belvedere. The last time before this that KH had reached the final was in 1907, and they have been in the final only once since.

I don't know why it was that only Protestant boys' schools played hockey. What was particularly 'Protestant' about the game I cannot say but KH always did well in hockey cup competitions. Maybe if Catholics wanted to play a game with a stick they played hurling. The way some KH boys, especially from the country, played hockey it was obvious they played hurling at home! None of the Protestant schools played Gaelic games but the head prefect in my second year, Jack Boothman, was in recent years President of the GAA, and another Blessington boy Billy Gobbett became a noted handballer. Sporting ecumenism thrives in West Wicklow.

Most Protestant schools played cricket as did, what might be called, the better Catholic schools. It is likely, however, that in these Catholic schools fewer boys played cricket than rugby, as the standard of cricket seemed to be roughly on a par with Protestant schools. Priests accompanied these teams, and the only other time I had seen priests at close quarters was on the street at home in Wexford. If I were with my Catholic friend Dick he would salute in a slightly obsequious way. I didn't salute because if I had Dick might think I was disrespectful but it never occurred to me that by not saluting, the priest probably thought that I was disrespectful.

Apart from that the first time I saw priests at close quarters was when they umpired cricket matches. They seemed to me to have an austere aura about them and these were the people who taught children that Protestants were going to hell. I wondered how they felt about their good Catholic boys playing against us. Was it one thing to beat the heretics, but was it a double humiliation to lose to them? I always had the feeling that while umpiring these mystical men, dressed entirely in black, would favour their own side when there was doubt about an appeal for lbw or a catch behind the wicket. I suppose I thought they would consider a member of the 'one-true-Church' entitled to the benefit of the doubt over a heretic. Such were my childish thoughts and I know these thoughts were unfair, and such were my own prejudices it never occurred to me that our own masters might well have unfairly favoured us.

I realise now that the belief of Roman Catholics that all Protestants were on their way to hell had a greater influence on me than I thought at the time. It was not that I thought it was true, I knew it was not true, and that whoever told the children who told me, in the various ways they did, including singing jingles across the street to that effect, was simply wrong. Nor was it that I was afraid of going to hell. In the first place I had no intention of dying and if I thought about it at all I'm sure I would have believed my death would be so far into the future that I had no need to think about it for years to come. Death to me was no more than funerals passing along the Main Street in Wexford. I had no concept of death. I had no concept of hell, nor, in fact, had I a concept of heaven. Nobody in my home, in church, in school or in Sunday School had ever spoken to me about heaven or hell, let alone made the threat of hell or held out the reward of heaven. On reflection both must have been mentioned in some shape or form in Bible stories I learned, but I had no sense that they applied to me.

The interesting question is: how did my Roman Catholic friends feel about playing with somebody who without doing anything bad in particular, other than the usual childish misdemeanours, was going to hell for no other reason than that he was a Protestant? Did they believe what their priests taught them? Did they feel sorry for Protestants? I think some did. Did they wonder why they couldn't attend the funeral service of a Protestant friend or neighbour? Did they resent this prohibition? I am simply curious to know how ordinary lay Roman Catholics of the time viewed the damnation of Protestants.

I saw no sign as a child that my Roman Catholic friends treated me any differently from anybody else. The fact that I was Protestant didn't seem to impinge in any way on my friendships. It arose only in passing perhaps because my friends didn't like to rub it in. It was never a subject for discussion, and if it had been, the only defence I had for not believing that we were all going to hell was that my mother had told me that that was nonsense. When I saw priests at close quarters, however, I didn't see them primarily as the perpetrators of offensive misinformation about Protestants. I saw them simply as authoritarian and inscrutable.

One cricket match we looked forward to every year was an all-day game for both junior and senior teams at Clongowes Wood. There was a bonus in that we missed morning class and got there in time for an 11 o'clock start. There were two cricket pitches, so both games took place simultaneously. Clongowes was a much posher school than ours. There were soutaned priests everywhere; umpiring, watching from the boundary and in the dining-hall when we went for lunch. From what I observed I had the impression that we were freer and less under discipline than the Clongowes boys. The whole atmosphere there seemed to me to be overtly religious and oppressive. This impression was caused in my mind by the presence of so many stern looking, black-clad priests from whom emanated an aura of authority. This seemed to say, 'I have the inside track on what God wants, it's a serious business, it's about sin, and if you enjoy yourself too much you are in danger of getting into sin. So don't enjoy yourself too much.'

At this time, in my early teens, the sum total of my religious education was stories of Jesus in the New Testament and of God in the Old Testament who spoke to people from the sky. The picture of Jesus I had was of a man who, in a way I didn't understand, was also God and who went around Palestine teaching and preaching to people to love God and to love each other and performing miracles. He was arrested, crucified, rose from the dead, the disciples saw him and then he ascended into heaven off the top of a mountain. After this the Holy Spirit came to the disciples. I had, in a simple way, a hold of all these basic teachings of the Christian faith from the New Testament.

The impression I had was that the Old Testament God-in-the-sky was a much more severe God than Jesus. I remember not thinking much of him making Abraham build a fire to sacrifice his son Isaac and stopping him at the last minute, just to test him out. I thought that was a lousy thing to do. As he was God did he not know exactly the extent of Abraham's faith?

There were two important religious ideas I picked up along the way. One was mainly from my home, which was to tell the truth at all costs and be honest in all my dealings. The second was that if you prayed to God well enough or often enough he would do what you asked; in effect, get you out of trouble. I can think of two occasions when as a boy I did this. One didn't work and the other did. He didn't help when I was homesick, but at the end of one term on the day before I was going home I discovered I was missing a gym shoe. I knew I would be in trouble when I got home if they had to buy me another pair. I would be told I was careless and that money to buy gym shoes didn't grow on trees. I prayed to God that I would find it. (I suppose if I had been a Catholic I would have prayed to St Anthony but I went straight to the top.) Right enough on the morning of the day that I was going home I found the shoe. When it turned up I remember the relief, but like the nine lepers I don't believe I said thanks to God.

At this stage of my life I accepted what my elders and betters told me concerning religious belief. I did not question it and I did not have the doubts about faith matters that I did as I grew up and in later life. Of one thing I am sure, amongst everything I learned about the Christian faith from my parents and from teachers, both primary and secondary, there wasn't a word about Protestants and Roman Catholics.

4

Vocation

When the Irish State was formed in 1922 one Catholic employee told her Protestant employer: 'Now yous'll be us and us'll be yous.'

Some Catholics in the south of Ireland saw Protestants in terms of their support for the former political establishment and presumably as privileged and well off. Even today a myth persists that there are no poor Protestants in the south, which of course is not true. Protestants are distributed through all strata of society.

My mother was in the home of a neighbour in Cork at around that time when a child of the house came in from school. The child's mother asked what he had learned at school.

'We learned to hate.'

'You learned to hate what?'

'Hate sin, hate the English and hate the Protestants.'

Some Protestants were told to their faces or had it daubed on their walls: 'Go home to where you belong', meaning England. Only a tiny minority of southern Protestants had any sense of England being their homeland. The great majority had no sense of belonging in England or in Northern Ireland. In many cases their families had been in Ireland for hundreds of years, and if the truth were known some of their families were here long before the families of those who thought they were more Irish because they were Roman Catholic. It was perfectly true that some Protestants were anti-Catholic and pro-British, but most were not.

Roman Catholicism and nationalism were closely bound together. Those who believed that in order to be properly Irish you had to be Roman Catholic did so despite the many Irish nationalist leaders that had been Protestant. Some Protestants were fearful of anti-Protestant attitudes and took them seriously. Others simply did not want to live in a Catholic dominated country because of the control exercised by the Catholic Church. Some Protestants, therefore, went to live in England or crossed the border into Northern Ireland. Many stayed because this was their home, they had nowhere else to go and they saw no reason why they should leave. Many who were involved in business stayed because to leave would have meant losing heavily financially. During the early years those that stayed, largely speaking, kept their heads down, while only a small number were active in the development of the new State.

Kevin O'Higgins, the State's first Minister for Justice, said in the Dáil in January 1922, referring to southern Protestants: '... it comes well from us to make a generous adjustment to show that these people are regarded, not as alien enemies, not as planters, but that we regard them as part and parcel of the nation, and that we wish them to take their share of its responsibilities.'

Depending on your perspective you might consider this unnecessarily patronising or sensitively reassuring. That he used the terms 'alien enemies' and 'planters', indicates how some people saw southern Irish Protestants at the time.

In 1955, thirty-three years later, when I left school, Protestants were largely unselfconscious citizens of the new State. Their numbers were so small that they were no threat to anybody and they lay so low they were barely noticed. Ireland at this time was a black and white society with green buses. There was a dearth of industry and an excess of religion. The economy was struggling to get on its feet, mass emigration was in full swing and the government and the Roman Catholic Church worked closely together.

The Most Reverend John Charles McQuaid was in his prime as Catholic Archbishop of Dublin. When he was President of Blackrock College he had been closely involved as an adviser to Eamon de Valera, the then Taoiseach, in drafting the 1937 Constitution, although de Valera, to his credit kept him in rein. In the constitution de Valera gave a 'special position' to the Catholic Church, 'as the guardian of the faith professed by the great majority of its citizens', and he gave recognition to named Protestant

Churches and the Jewish community. As recently as the previous century the Roman Catholic Church proscribed the granting of recognition to other Christian Churches and imposed sanctions where it could on the Jewish community. No doubt it would have pleased Archbishop McQuaid more if de Valera had designated Catholicism the State religion, but he didn't. Now as Archbishop of Dublin Archbishop McQuaid was prepared to extinguish any liberal development that stirred. In common with the rest of the Catholic hierarchy, among whom he was the dominant figure, he opposed anything that did not conform to a conservative interpretation of Roman Catholic teaching.

The subservience of the government to the Catholic Church was seen in the behaviour of the Coalition Government formed in 1948. After their first cabinet meeting, the Minister for External Affairs, Seán MacBride, sent a telegram to the Pope on behalf of the government, affirming its willingness: 'To repose at the feet of Your Holiness the assurance of our filial loyalty and our devotion to Your August Person as well as our firm resolve to be guided in all our work by the teaching of Christ and to strive for the attainment of a social order in Ireland based on Christian principles.' (McBride had sent an even more obsequious letter to Archbishop McQuaid on his own election to the Dáil the previous year.)

It was as Joyce had said:

O Ireland my first and only love
Where Christ and Caesar are hand and glove!

In 1951, true to its word, the government acceded to pressure from the Catholic bishops and withdrew a bill giving healthcare to mothers and children because the bishops deemed it to be contrary to Catholic social teaching. After much bitterness, complicated by his fraught relationship with his party leader Seán MacBride, the Minister for Health, Dr Noel Browne, not having the support of the Taoiseach and the rest of the government eventually resigned and published the correspondence in *The Irish Times*. This affair gave rise to a highly charged controversy on Church/State relations.

The Catholic Church had a position on everything and imposed it when it could. They even had a position on the use of women's sanitary wear. Archbishop McQuaid told the government of the Church's disapproval of the sale of tampons. The bishops feared they could stimulate young girls who might become sexually aroused and even use contraceptives while satisfying their arousal. For a time the government prohibited their sale. Can you imagine how Protestants, especially women, viewed the interference of elderly male celibate bishops in such a matter?

By 1955, apart from isolated incidents, Protestants were, largely speaking, comfortable in the now Republic, despite the fact that they lived in a country in which the ethos and some of the laws reflected the religious values of the 95 per cent majority of the population. They lived in a society that believed a minority, especially such a small one, should expect to have to live with the values and attitudes of the majority. Catholic teaching through social policy was imposed on Protestants, members of other faiths and non-believers, not that there were many of the latter in those days. Divorce and artificial contraception were not available to people who might want them. Catholic teaching on abortion made some women fearful that if things went wrong medically at delivery the baby might be saved at the expense of the mother. Consequently it was not unknown for an expectant mother, especially if there was reason to have a particular anxiety, to go to Northern Ireland, or to England if she could afford it, to have her baby. State censorship of books, that reflected a conservative Roman Catholic position, meant that some of the works of the best Irish and international writers were banned and not available in Ireland. In fact it used to be said that any Irish writer worth his or her salt was banned.

Protestants were forced to live with all of these restrictions. If they wanted contraception or divorce at an appropriate time in their lives they simply weren't available. This was not a constant preoccupation of Protestants in the Republic, but Protestants were conscious that the laws of the land forced them to conform to Catholic teaching on these issues. Among Protestants, however, there were many who were as opposed to divorce as Roman Catholics were.

The Protestant in the pew might ask why the Catholic Church felt the need to have these matters enforced by the laws of the State? Why did they not simply proscribe them for their own members by Church law in the same way they forbade the eating of meat on a Friday, or attendance at Protestant religious services? This would allow Protestants and others whose consciences did not forbid these things, to avail of them. I assume the answer would be that these were moral issues that the Catholic Church, believing itself to be the One True Church, had exclusive insight into and control over, and it was the Church's duty to impose them even on non-Roman Catholics for their own good. The Protestant would then want to ask what merit there is for Roman Catholics in being moral when there is no opportunity to be immoral, making a virtue of necessity, as compared with being moral when there is freedom to choose. Is there any merit in not contravening the moral law when there is no opportunity to contravene it; a matter of imposed morality as opposed to morality freely chosen?'

Nonetheless at this time I did not feel that I lived in a state of subjection, but then I did not need contraceptives, divorce or tampons. I did feel, and I believe that this was felt by many Protestants, that the Roman Catholic Church, from its own perception of its unique relationship with God and supported by the government, considered me, and all non-Roman Catholics, morally inferior beings. When I thought about it, and this wasn't often at the time, this did not bother me. I was in no doubt that nobody, not even the Catholic Church, had a right to make the judgement that a person was morally superior or inferior to anybody else. That was a matter for God. Anybody had a right to say they believed that a particular act was moral or immoral. Anybody had a right to say what they believed to be right or wrong on such moral issues, but not to invoke the law of the land to impose their view on those who disagreed. This was the Roman Catholic dominated Ireland in which I took my place when I left school.

My father had died when I was in third form. This event changed completely the course of my family life. My sister went to England and joined the WRAF and my mother and I left Wexford and moved to Monkstown, Co Dublin. At the end of fourth form when I had done the Intermediate Certificate I had convinced my mother that I should leave school and I launched myself into the wicked world. I have no doubt that, given my poor academic performance at school, my mother was convinced that it was preferable that I should begin to make my way in the world rather than waste any further the time of those who tried to teach me, or the money on school fees.

The day-to-day image of Roman Catholicism I, as a young Protestant, had was naturally based on the public face of the Church – the many priests and nuns that one saw in public. Priests dressed wholly in black sometimes read their breviaries on buses or trains or even walking along the street. I had the impression that they saw themselves as witnesses to the seriousness of a religion that did not allow even a modicum of levity. They seemed to invite deference and their acknowledgement of other people in public was more likely to be a dignified forward inclination of the head than speech. I don't know if it was a Protestant joke or if it was shared by Catholics, that Ireland was the only country in the world where on a bus a pregnant woman would stand up to let a priest sit down.

Whereas Protestant clergy wore clerical collars and more often grey rather than black suits, we had no friars or nuns, at least not that I knew of – I was surprised to learn later on that there was a convent of Anglican nuns in Sandymount. The friars seemed to be much more relaxed then the priests. The nuns had huge headdresses and full skirts to the ground, and from within what was virtually a personal tent, only face and hands were visible. Both friars and nuns had hanging from their belts one of the symbols of Catholicism and entirely foreign to me – rosary beads.

There was little doubt which church buildings were Catholic and which Protestant. The Catholic ones were usually much bigger; apart from the two Dublin Cathedrals, they tended to be of later vintage and of course the 'giveaway' was statues in the grounds outside. Walking along the street, or on a bus passing a Catholic church Catholics made the sign of the cross. One night a friend and I, having missed the last bus from town, were hitching to Monkstown and a priest stopped and gave us a lift. When we passed what was then the new church on Merrion Road the priest made the sign of the cross. We followed suit in order not to draw attention to the fact that we were Protestants, not that we thought he would put us out of the car if he knew, but simply to avoid what we thought might be an awkward situation.

The sight of a crocodile of young boys dressed entirely in black and wearing black soft hats, out for a walk with a priest or priests behind them keeping a watchful eye further reminded the Protestant observer of the all-pervasive position of the Catholic Church. The presence of priests or bishops, often robed, on public and civic occasions left nobody in any doubt that this was a Catholic country. The sight of people going down on one knee to kiss a bishop's ring reminded Protestants, if they needed reminding, of the power and status of the Catholic Church in southern Ireland.

There were all kinds of subtle ways to determine if a person was Catholic or Protestant. The most obvious was to ascertain to which school they went. Protestants were far more likely to read *The Irish Times,* and even dead ones were discernible by the absence of RIP and usually the presence of a quotation from a hymn or the Bible in their death notices. The Protestant eye scanning the death columns of *The Irish Times* was adept at discerning the demise of one of their own. In the experience of one undertaker the practice of quoting the age of the deceased, when they had lived to a good age, as 'in their such and such year', rather than simply giving their age last birthday is a Protestant idiosyncrasy!

Since Gaelic games were not played in Protestant schools, not many Protestant young people played either hurling or Gaelic football. Those few who did were likely to have lived in the country and to have attended local Technical or Catholic Schools. Years later, some short time after I went as rector to a country parish, I attended the local GAA dinner as a guest with the parish priest. Not only was there a good representation of the Church of Ireland community there, but I was particularly pleased to see three of my young parishioners going up to receive medals as members of a cup-winning team.

For some people not only had one to be a Roman Catholic to be a proper Irishman, but one had to play Gaelic games, and most Protestants failed on both counts. Some would say that there was a third qualification for a proper Irishman: to be a member of that third prominent institution of Irish society, Fianna Fáil, and most Prods would fail on this one too, but that's another day's work.

In 1951 Wexford reached the All Ireland hurling final for the first time since they won the championship in 1910. Tipperary won, but this was the beginning of a resurgence of hurling in Wexford. They lost to Cork in 1954 and won the title in 1955 and 1956. Any boy from Wexford of any religion or sporting allegiance, or of none, would have had to have a heart of stone not to have been caught up in the euphoria of those years. As only a sports-keen schoolboy can, I could name every member of the team and every score line and give every detail of every championship. The year after I left school, 1956, Wexford defended the championship and being no longer subject to the constraints of boarding school I went to the final.

There is no finer sporting spectacle than a good game of top-class hurling. It is the fastest field sport in the world. The speed and skill of the game at senior level are pure magic. The final of 1956 was one such game. The three Rackard brothers were playing for Wexford and Christy Ring was playing for Cork. With the possible exception of Mick Mackey of Limerick of earlier years, Ring was considered the greatest hurler who ever played. Not only was he a master of hurling but he was also a master of gamesmanship, a deadly combination. In the 1956 final one particular incident showed him to be a good sportsman. At a critical point in the game he slipped his marker and drove a pile-driver of a shot at the Wexford goal at close range and Art Foley, the Wexford keeper, by instinct put up his hand and miraculously the ball stuck. He cleared the ball and Christy Ring ran in and shook him by the hand.

Inevitably there were more Cork supporters at Croke Park that day than Wexford supporters. It was well known that Dublin was full of Cork people and it was rumoured in those days that Glanmire, the main railway station in Cork, sold only one-way tickets to Dublin! Furthermore, Cork people were considered the Aberdonians of Ireland; tight with money, and Dubliners believed they kept them out of all the best jobs. At half time there came an announcement over the public address system: 'A purse has been found containing a small sum of money and a return ticket to Cork ...' the crowd erupted with laughter that drowned out the rest of the announcement.

Having worked for a little over a year as a clerk in Brittain's motor assembly plant at Portobello Bridge I moved to an insurance company in College Green in 1956. It was a small life insurance company with eleven employees. The boss's secretary, like many a boss's secretary, was older and wiser than the average secretary and she was loyal and able. As a person she was well-read, reflective and a non-practising Protestant. She used to have discussions from time to time with one of the inspectors, a Catholic whose father, a former Protestant, had converted to Catholicism on his marriage. The inspector was an avid Catholic who believed the Roman Catholic Church to be the One True Church and the Pope its infallible head. He was a staunch defender of the Roman Catholic faith and of the Church's position on everything.

I was present on one occasion for a discussion between these two (they were both too civilised to have an argument) about the authority of the Pope. The secretary presented the case that the reputation of the Pope was, to say the least, tarnished by the fact that in 1935 he blessed Italian Air Force planes before they went off to bomb the Abyssinians. She claimed to know her facts because she was reading a book on the subject at the time. The inspector was flummoxed by this information and could only justify it on the grounds that if the Pope had done it, it must have been the right thing to do. The respective attitudes of these two drew my attention for the first time in a clear way to the opposing characteristics of the way Protestants and Catholics think. The Protestant will be inclined to work things out for herself and in the end make up her own mind on an issue. The Catholic will start from the position that the Church is right in all its thoughts, words and deeds and if the Church says or does something it must be right, and it's not for uninformed laity to think for themselves on matters that the Church has decided upon. Religious discussions in those days were almost always debates of the relevant merits of the authority and the doctrinal positions of the different institutional Churches, and not about matters of belief itself.

This particular inspector used to tell us stories from his early days collecting weekly Industrial Life Assurance premiums from tenement houses in Dublin in the late 1940s. The business was often conducted from the street to an upstairs window, and more than once women had offered him favours in lieu of the weekly premium. On one occasion having threatened that if the premium were not paid the policy would lapse he turned to go and was struck on the back of the head by a cabbage stump. He used to tell us that we young fellows didn't know how well off we were working in a comfortable, centrally-heated office where premiums arrived by cheque in the post.

When I was a child some Roman Catholic children had solemnly informed me that Protestants did not believe in purgatory. Had I been smart enough I might have replied that since they thought that Protestants were all going straight to hell anyway, we had no need to believe in purgatory, but needless to say I didn't. I was aware that Catholics prayed for the souls in purgatory, but until I worked in this insurance company I had no idea what kind of money was sometimes involved. It was necessary for the will of a deceased policyholder to be submitted to the company to be noted before the claim was paid. In reading these wills I was astounded at the sums of money that people left to priests to have Masses said for the repose of their souls. It wasn't just a few pounds, it was often hundreds, when a hundred pounds was a substantial sum, and sometimes it was even thousands. These legacies usually came first, before legacies to family. As an uninformed Protestant it looked to me that a person could buy their way into heaven and that it gave the well-off an unfair advantage over the poor. That the rich had an advantage over the poor in this world I took for granted, but that such advantage should extend into the next world surprised me.

As a child it somehow didn't occur to me as strange to see Catholics making the sign of the cross passing a church, though I didn't understand its significance. I was somewhat puzzled however when my friends made the sign of the cross before they went into the water to swim. I assumed that it was a way of asking God to keep them safe from drowning. I did not learn this kind of understanding of God in my own religious upbringing. Without being told in so many words I learned that my safety when swimming was my own responsibility. Swim where it is known to be safe, don't swim for at least an hour after a meal, don't swim out of your depth unless you are a strong swimmer and don't lark about in the water. It seemed strange to me that people believed that God would intervene to keep them safe from danger while swimming, despite the fact that there was a prayer with a similar sentiment in the evening service of the Church of Ireland prayer book. It asked God to 'defend us from all perils and dangers of this night'. That prayer was composed long before the advent of electric light when darkness was more threatening than it is today. Electricity went a long way towards banishing ghosts and the perils and dangers of the night.

On 2 December 1956 Ronnie Delaney won the 1500 metres at the Melbourne Olympics. This was, rightly, a matter of great national pride. He was only the third Irishman to win an Olympic gold medal in track and field competition. The previous two were Pat O'Callaghan in 1928 and 1932 for throwing the hammer, and Bob Tisdall in 1932 for 400 metre hurdles. There was a civic reception for Delaney when he arrived back in Dublin airport and he was driven through the streets of Dublin in the back of an open-topped car. From the office in College Green where I worked we watched through the window as the crowds clapped him as he passed.

The thing that intrigued me, however, was that when we saw the newsreel of the race when Delaney breasted the tape to win, the first thing he did was to bless himself, kneel down on the track and pray. I wondered what he said. Did he thank God for helping him to win the race? Did he thank God he had won the race?

If it was either of these might God not have had divided loyalty if other runners had also prayed for help. Would it have been a matter of God helping the one who prayed hardest to him before the race? Or by what other criterion might God have helped one competitor rather than the other? Did God have a hand in the race at all?

Surely Delaney won the race because he was the best athlete on the day; he was the fastest and employed the right tactics. I do not wish to be disrespectful to Delaney or to God, but I think the person to be thanked was his coach and other people who helped him to prepare. I have no doubt he did thank these people, but I cannot understand why he would pray to God immediately he won. Does God involve himself in helping people at sport? I have no doubt that there are Protestants who believe he does and would pray in a similar way to Delaney in the same circumstances. Nothing in my religious upbringing gave me reason to believe that sport is an area in which God intervenes. I noticed watching recent football world cup matches that some players blessed themselves before taking penalties. If the goalkeeper blessed himself would that neutralise that or what do these players understand themselves to be doing when they invoke the Holy Trinity in penalty shots and what would be the Church's position on it?

In 1957 the notorious controversy in the small south Co Wexford village of Fethard-on-Sea erupted. A Church of Ireland mother in a mixed marriage told the parish priest she would not send her daughter to the local Catholic school when she came to school-going age. She reneged on the promise to bring her children up as Catholics that she had made before her marriage. When pressure was put on her she went away with her two daughters to Northern Ireland and then to Scotland. Rumour circulated that Protestants locally had encouraged the girls' mother to take them away. The local Protestants denied this strenuously. I am sure they had an opinion one way or the other, but they would have considered it a matter for the family. As a result of the rumour Catholics boycotted local Protestant shops and the Catholic sexton in one of the local Church of Ireland churches was put under pressure to leave his job. Understandably these events polarised local opinion along religious lines, and it soon became a national controversy. It was discussed in the Dáil, in the Northern Ireland Parliament and in the foreign press. To his great credit de Valera stood up in the Dáil and condemned the boycott and called for it to be brought to a speedy end. The wife's father appealed for her to come home and the parish priest ended the boycott by buying a packet of cigarettes in a Protestant shop. The mother and the girls returned to Fethard and the parents resolved the problem of the girls' education by teaching them at home.

I have no doubt it is difficult for ordinary Roman Catholics to understand how unjust the promise required on entering a mixed marriage at that time was to Protestants. Before this promise was required under the *Ne Temere* Decree of 1907, the custom was that boys were brought up in their father's religion and girls in their mother's religion. This was a fair arrangement as, in the nature of things, proportions would balance out. The inflexible application of *Ne Temere* perpetrated an appalling injustice against the Protestant community, especially in the south of Ireland where by 1957 they were in such a small minority anyway. The Church required the promise to be made before the marriage when a couple, madly in love, would promise almost anything to get on with the marriage. The reality of the promise only arose when the first baby arrived, often many years later, and this frequently caused mayhem in the family. It was often the grandparents of the new baby that were the problem, putting pressure on their children, implicit or explicit, to secure their grandchild for their own religion.

Be it said that in Orthodox Tsarist Russia towards the end of the nineteenth century something similar pertained, enforced by the state. In the case of a marriage between a member of the Orthodox Church and a member of another religion, it was illegal, according to the law of the land, for the children to follow the religion of the non-Orthodox parent. There were instances where children were taken forcibly from 'heretic' parents when they refused to bring them up in the Orthodox faith.

It is perfectly understandable that a strongly believing Roman Catholic would want to bring up his or her children as Catholics, but why could such a person not understand that his or her strongly believing Protestant partner would want to do the same? The Protestant would consider it a matter for the couple themselves, without interference from outside, to work out how they would bring up their children. I believe that the Protestant resentment of the Catholic Church's interference in their marriage was not so much on matters of doctrine, though this may have been the case with some, but rather it was resentment at the interference of the Church in their private lives. Protestants were incredulous of the control exercised by the Catholic Church, especially in intimate matters. Furthermore, apart from official prohibitions, Protestants in a mixed marriage would know of the influence that priests had over their people, and be fearful that such influence would be brought to bear on their spouse. It was not unknown for a priest to visit the family of a mixed marriage and drop hints, or say explicitly, that it was about time that they had another child. Protestants would consider this an outrageous intrusion into the private life of the couple.

In those days there was a story about a Protestant who had become a Roman Catholic to please his future wife. He told the priest how hard he found it to believe that he was now a Catholic.

'When you feel like that,' the priest said, 'just keep repeating to yourself: "I'm a Catholic, not a Protestant, I'm a Catholic not a Protestant …"' After the couple were married a few months, one Friday evening the priest thought he'd call to see how they were getting on. As the wife let him in he noticed a strong smell of meat frying. When he entered the kitchen there was the husband flipping a big juicy steak in the pan, saying: 'You're a fish not a steak, you're a fish not a steak …'

Eamon de Valera was admired for his call for an end to the Fethard-on-Sea boycott. He was, after all, a national politician and international statesman. At one stage he had been president of the League of Nations. It is incredible, therefore, that later on when he was President of Ireland, before he accepted an invitation to review a Protestant Boys' Brigade event, he felt he had to consult Archbishop McQuaid as to whether he could or not. The Church of Ireland Archbishop, George Simms, was due to give the blessing. Archbishop McQuaid replied that it would be lawful for the President to attend provided he took no active part in the proceedings, and so de Valera promised not to take his hat off during the ceremony!

The liberal brand of Protestantism I was brought up in did not include trying to convert anybody, least of all Roman Catholics to Protestantism. I had heard of Catholics trying to convert Protestants, especially on the occasion of mixed marriages, and there had been an occasion in Wexford when there was a furore when the nuns at the convent had angled to convert a Protestant pupil. I suppose a good Catholic would genuinely hope to save a Protestant, particularly one they liked, from hell, by wanting them to convert to Catholicism. I had not, however, heard of Protestants trying to convert Catholics, as nobody had ever suggested to me that Catholics would by definition not qualify for eternal life.

Consequently I found it strange, after I left school, when I first encountered some evangelical Protestants who did think that Roman Catholics were all so mistaken in their beliefs that they had no chance of salvation. I discovered that there was even a Protestant Mission whose purpose it was to convert Roman Catholics, in order to save their souls. In this matter of trying to gain converts there were those in both religions who were as bad as each other.

There was in the 1950s, and even later, a brand of evangelical Protestant, not attached to any of the main-line churches, who used to preach on the street. They came from the YMCA in Abbey Street and preached standing on a box, soap or other I don't know, at Elephant House, Elvery's Corner, at the junction of O'Connell Street and Middle Abbey Street. On summer evenings they preached at the bottom of Marine Road, Dun Laoghaire, in the hope of making converts from among the strollers to and from the East Pier.

These were people who had had strong emotional conversion experiences themselves and believed that anybody, Catholic or

Protestant alike, who hadn't had a similar religious experience, was destined for hell. Baptism and active membership of a Church wasn't enough. They reinforced their conviction by the use of texts from the Bible that they quoted liberally and selectively in their preaching and issued challenges to all and sundry to give their lives to the Lord or face eternal damnation. They certainly didn't attract crowds, but occasionally a few people might stop and listen for a while. From time to time youngsters passing would shout a comment or two but generally speaking they were well tolerated and nobody interfered with them. They were something like a Protestant equivalent of the Legion of Mary who distributed tracts on the street. The Legion, however, comported themselves with greater discretion.

I saw the Roman Catholic Church as a monolith, the clergy as stern disciplinarians and the people as a compliant and obedient flock conforming to hierarchical and ultimately absolute papal authority. I believed there was no room for diversity within its membership; that all Roman Catholics believed exactly the same things in the same way and accepted every detail of doctrine as taught to them in school. This in contrast to the variety within Protestantism, from the Church of Ireland at one end through Presbyterian and Methodist to the YMCA preachers at the other end.

Bigotry is not the exclusive preserve of any one religion. There are bigoted members of all religions. I once expressed surprise to a Protestant, a man much older than me, that Seán O'Casey was a Protestant, probably because his names were not typically Protestant, not knowing it was a *nom de plume*. His reply was: 'Of course he was a Protestant. Wasn't anybody who was ever any good a Protestant?' I was dumbfounded. This man was a southern Protestant born and bred, and in my experience such bigotry in the south was rare. O'Casey gave typical Protestant names to his tenement dwelling Protestant, Bessie Burgess.

Despite the fact that Dublin was probably one of the most Catholic cities in the world, for two successive years it did not have a Catholic Lord Mayor. Between 1960–1961 Maurice Dockrell, a

Fine Gael Protestant, and 1961–1962, Robert Briscoe, a Fianna
Fáil Jew, were Lord Mayors. Briscoe had already held the office in
1956-1957. One cannot help wondering what Archbishop John
Charles McQuaid thought of this. It was bad enough a Protes-
tant, but a Jew, a member of the race considered by the Catholic
Church guilty of deicide, must have been hard for him to swallow.
The Roman Catholic Good Friday liturgy pre-Second Vatican
Council still referred to Jews as 'perfidious', while a collect in the
Church of Ireland liturgy of Good Friday prays:

> Have mercy upon thine ancient people Israel, and all who know not
> thee as revealed in the Gospel of thy Son; take from them all igno-
> rance, hardness of heart, and contempt of thy Word; and so fetch
> them home, blessed Lord, to thy fold, that they may be made one
> flock under one Shepherd, Jesus Christ our Lord ...

The Church of Ireland has a society that was called: 'The Church's
Mission to the Jews.' It was renamed recently, 'The Church's Ministry
Among Jews.' It's my opinion they should leave the Jews alone.

1961 was the 1,500th anniversary of the death of St Patrick. A
Patrician Congress was arranged and the year declared a Patrician
year. Cardinal Agagianian, believed to have been the 'underbidder'
when Pope John XXIII had been elected, came to Dublin as representative of the Vatican. Amongst the dignitaries who were at the
airport to meet him was the Lord Mayor. It was the custom at the
time for Catholics greeting a bishop or cardinal to kneel and kiss
his ring, and so Maurice Dockrell, a Protestant amongst whom
there was no such custom, knelt and kissed the cardinal's ring.
There was a furore amongst some Protestants who felt he betrayed
Protestantism to Catholic triumphalism. Mr Dockrell defended
himself simply and effectively on the grounds that he was not
greeting the cardinal in his personal capacity, but on behalf of the
citizens of Dublin, 95 per cent or more of whom were Catholics.
He came out of the controversy well and left the begrudging Protestants with egg on their faces.

For many of these years after I left school I took little interest
in matters religious, although I continued to go to church with

my mother on Sundays. I worked for a modest wage, studied for insurance exams, played rugby and cricket, winter and summer. After five or six years of an active sporting life and of even more active participation in the social scene that goes with it, involving copious quantities of pints and parties on Saturday nights and into Sunday mornings, the hectic times started to pall. I began to reflect. It would be pretentious in the extreme to say that I asked questions about the meaning of life, but I did wonder where it was all leading. As time passed my experience of the world, limited though it was, turned me towards some serious consideration of the human condition, its nature and destiny. Naturally I would not have used such a grandiloquent way of saying so, but I did begin in a simple way to ask questions about what I was doing and where I was going and what it was all about.

Slowly I developed a sense of vocation to ordination. Why and how I cannot explain, but it was unmistakable. Many years later I learned that in a survey of clergy in the Presbyterian Church in Scotland, 70 per cent of those surveyed about their vocations had lost their fathers by death or desertion or had lost emotional contact with their fathers, by the age of fourteen. I was fourteen when my father died. Whether I try to account for my religious vocation theologically or psychologically or as a mixture of the two, there it was, and it was real. I did have a clear sense that it came from God – about whom I knew very little.

On reflection my vocation did not contain a strong sense of the issue of salvation, i.e. that the purpose of life was to avoid hell and to get to heaven. I was taught nothing of this kind of religion in my home or in school. I was taught about living life honourably and truthfully according to the principle, inculcated into me as a child, to tell the truth and shame the devil, though I knew even less about him than I knew about God. The abiding maxim of my childhood religious education, however, was to 'do unto others as you would they should do unto you.'

I consulted the relevant Church authorities, who, as the result of a thorough selection process, confirmed that I did indeed have a vocation to ordination. To use that phrase beloved these days of lawyers and politicians, 'after due process' in Michaelmas term, October 1962, I entered Trinity College, Dublin, to study for a degree as a preliminary to a course of training for ordination in the Church of Ireland. A week or two earlier on 11 October the Second Vatican Council, called by Pope John XXIII, who on succeeding to the Papacy had said: 'Here I am at the end of the road and at the top of the heap', met for the first time. There were changes ahead for the Catholic Church, and for me.

5

University

The first few years of the 1960s saw the beginnings of change in Irish society. This change was brought about, no doubt, by the co-incidence of many factors but there were some clearly identifiable events that were significant in the development of a more open society. Telefís Éireann was established in 1960 which meant that many aspects of Irish life were held up to public scrutiny in a way that radio had not done. Until then there was only English television in Ireland pirated from Wales and Northern Ireland. A particular catalyst for change was the *Late Late Show*. Gay Byrne was fearless in bringing onto the show topics that had not been discussed on the airwaves in Ireland before. Though officially a light entertainment programme he aired political, religious and sexual topics in a way that slew many sacred cows and created controversy. He brought guests with liberal and conservative views on these topics onto the programme and gave ordinary members of the audience an opportunity to express their views. Many of these discussions gave rise to debate that extended into the letters pages of the national newspapers and in some cases lasted for weeks.

A Catholic bishop phoned the show one Saturday night outraged that Gay Byrne should mention the nightdress a participant wore on her honeymoon. The woman herself suggested that she might not have worn a nightdress at all. It was just a bit of fun and should some Protestants have considered it to be in bad taste they would not have considered it a matter in which a bishop should intervene. The controversy revealed that many Catholics thought the same, but many agreed with the bishop. There was great amusement one night when Oliver Flanagan, a conservative Catholic and member of the Dáil, told the nation that there was no sex in Ireland before television. Everybody knew exactly what he meant but some used the way he expressed it to ridicule the poor man. Fr Fergal O'Connor, a lecturer in UCD, was a frequent guest on the show and expressed liberal views that were often not in line with the Catholic Church authorities.

There was a sense in which Protestants watched from the sideline as Catholics came to terms one way or another with the consequences for their religion of the development of this liberal trend. Protestants too had to come to terms with some of these developments, but their Churches, in the main, would have left such matters for them to decide for themselves according to their consciences. It seems to Protestants that the Catholic Church has a law for everything and Catholics are accountable to God through the clergy and the Church for how they behave and their beliefs. Members of the Protestant Churches learn the gospel principles as taught by Jesus in the New Testament and believe themselves to be accountable directly to God for their beliefs and behaviour.

In 1963 John F. Kennedy visited Ireland. JFK was the first Roman Catholic President of the United States. He was young and his election signalled great hope and expectation for America and the western world. His Irish Catholic background was a matter of great pride in Ireland and it was not uncommon in Irish homes at the time to see his photograph hanging beside that of the Pope. Southern Irish Protestants, while naturally not having the same sense of his Catholicism as their Catholic neighbours, shared their pride in his Irishness. He stayed in Ireland for three days, addressed the Dáil and visited cousins and the site of his ancestral home in Co Wexford. Five months after his visit he was assassinated.

In due course Ireland was badly let down when it transpired that John Kennedy's marriage was not what it appeared, and that he had had several affairs, most notoriously with Marilyn Monroe, and had used prostitutes when staying away from home. The name of the Kennedy family was further besmirched when Bobbie Kennedy was alleged to have been involved in a cover-up to do with Marilyn Monroe's death. It was also alleged that Ted Kennedy had some responsibility for the death of a young woman, Mary Jo Kopechnie, in a car crash at Chapaquiddick, near a Kennedy family retreat.

In 1963 the Beatles came to Dublin. They came to perform in the conservative Catholic ethos of a Dublin still under the firm control of Archbishop McQuaid. I remember feeling at the time that older people would see the hysterical enthusiasm with which Dublin's young people received them, as an aberration from pagan England and that when they went back things in Holy Ireland would return to normal. This, of course, did not happen. Rather it was the beginning of what are now called the swinging 1960s.

Every year, when the Lenten Pastoral Letters of the Catholic bishops were published in the national newspapers, it was as certain as that night follows day that Archbishop McQuaid included in his letter a reiteration of the prohibition on the attendance of Catholics at Trinity College, Dublin. This was frequently mentioned in the pastorals of other diocesan bishops too.

Trinity was founded in 1592 and granted a charter by Queen Elizabeth I. It had been a bastion of the Irish Protestant Ascendancy in its day and of its brand of Low Church Protestantism. The Catholic Church had denounced Trinity for many years as a place unsuitable for the education of Catholics. Archbishop McQuaid went one step further and forbade Catholics of his diocese to attend Trinity, on pain of mortal sin, unless by his special permission, which he granted only in exceptional circumstances. He seemed to have a 'thing' about Trinity and must surely have felt miffed when in 1956 Seán T. O'Kelly, a Knight of Columbanus and a particularly pious Catholic, then President of Ireland, accepted an honorary degree from the university.

From the Protestant point of view this prohibition was yet another instance of the Catholic Church saying something like: 'We are the One True Church, we have unique access to absolute truth. We do not allow our members to be present at Protestant worship lest they be attracted to something that is heretical. We do not allow our members to attend your schools or universities either, because to do so might endanger their faith. As Protestants you are heretics and going to hell and if we allow Catholics to go to Trinity they will be in danger of freedom of thought, perhaps adopt some heresy and end up in hell too.'

I believe that this is a fair representation of the Protestant understanding of how the Catholic Church viewed them. I also believe that Protestants were not in the slightest bit bothered by what the Roman Catholic Church thought of them. Protestants would consider hell, if they believed in it at all, a place or state of being for people who have perpetrated serious evil, a place for people of wilful depravity. They might wonder if this is what Roman Catholics really think of us, people of such evil, simply because we believe in and worship the same God in some ways differently from them. Are we really that bad in the sight of Roman Catholics?

Many Protestants would, I believe, have made a distinction in their minds between what the Roman Catholic Church taught and what they understood their Catholic friends and neighbours might think. Catholic friends and neighbours did not treat them as despised heretical wretches destined for hell, though I know that some Catholics did have difficulty reconciling what they knew and liked or admired about their Protestant friends with what their Church taught about them. The effect of reminding a Protestant from an early age that they are going to hell is to imply that they are worthless. Their crime is what they believe, not what they have done. It is therefore bound to colour their view of the people who tell them this and of the institution, the Roman Catholic Church, behind the assertion.

In the Michaelmas term, October 1962, I entered Trinity to study for a degree as a preliminary to studying for ordination. Trinity contained the divinity school that trained ordinands for the Church of Ireland. This together with the academic freedom of the university at large, were of course the reasons for the Catholic Church's fear of it. Put simply a university that had a Protestant ethos, a Protestant divinity school and unfettered academic freedom was to the Catholic Church a serious threat to the faith and morals of ordinary Roman Catholics, and the Church must protect them from it.

Having left school when I was fifteen I was pleased at the opportunity, late though I was, to go to university and I was determined to make the most of it. Boys from my secondary school went every year to Trinity and an uncle and cousin were graduates. Trinity was very much part of the Protestant world in which I had been brought up and it was quite natural that I should go there. I had no sense whatever of the Roman Catholic estimate of it as a dangerous place. Talking to some Roman Catholic students later on they said that they encountered nothing in Trinity that was a threat to their faith and morals.

What was striking, however, was the high proportion of English students. In 1963 the number of English students was at its peak at one third of the student population. Many of these had gone to English public schools and having failed to gain entrance to Oxford or Cambridge they came to Trinity. Some of these English students were well off, drove cars, even sports cars, and lived the high life. One day in the Reading Room I sat beside one of them I knew from lectures. He was bemoaning the fact that he had lost money at the races the previous afternoon. I noted that what he had lost was a sum greater than that which my mother and I lived on for a month! English students contributed greatly to college life and some stayed in Ireland after graduation. Others became well-known names as writers, actors and media personalities in England. Some however gave the impression they were slightly amused at being at university with the native Irish. Approximately 10 per cent of the student body was from Northern Ireland and 10 per cent or more came from abroad. This mix made for a cosmopolitan air about the college that was never short of interest.

I was staid, dull and older than the average student and I couldn't help but be amused by the loud and often disruptive behaviour of some students. It was as though this was the way to behave authentically at university. Some went a stage further and were practised exhibitionists and one girl, Rosemary Gibson, didn't seem to be able to walk across Front Square without causing a commotion and attracting attention to herself. The height of her notoriety came one day when she jumped into the Liffey to rescue a dog. Her heroic deed was headline news in one of the evening papers. There is no doubt this kind of behaviour was part of your average Dubliner's image of Trinity students at the time: wild, exhibitionist and probably a teeny-weeny bit lax in the moral department. This image was summed up expressively by one of the women, a true Dub, who cleared the tables in the buttery and always ended the conversation with: 'Yeuse steudents is all the same.'

I suppose it was inevitable that given the route by which I arrived in Trinity, the desire to be ordained in the Church of Ireland, I should find myself in the company of students with the same purpose. The focal point for ordinands were the rooms of the College Theological Society in East Chapel, beside the steps to the dining hall, but while working for a degree, before theological studies, I was determined not to be sucked into the exclusive company of divinity students. However, the 'Theo' rooms were a handy place to sit and read the paper, to have a warm at the fire on a cold day, and to leave a coat or books while at lectures or in the reading room, or anywhere else for that matter. For these conveniences I joined the 'Theo' and discovered amongst its membership, almost all ordinands, a diverse group of men. At this stage membership of the society was exclusively male and Anglican. There were, however, a few female camp-followers. An aspiring cleric was a respectable specimen to bring home to one's mother; he might become a dean or archdeacon or even a bishop!

The Church of Ireland, like the other main Churches, is an all-Ireland Church. Since over three quarters of its members live in Northern Ireland and less than one quarter in the Republic, and its only Divinity School for training ordinands is in Dublin, it is inevitable that the Divinity School would have more northern than southern students. And since the 'Theo' was where Church of Ireland ordinands in Trinity hung out I met more northerners than southerners there.

My experience of the Church of Ireland up to this time had been in Wexford, a provincial town parish, the chapel at school,

The King's Hospital, and Monkstown, Co Dublin, a suburban parish. All were similar: broad church and middle class. In the 'Theo' I met for the first time men planning to be ordained in the Church of Ireland that were not broad church, middle class, and from the south, but evangelical, working class and from the north. No matter how I express this difference somebody is going to take offence, either on theological, social or even political grounds. I'm sorry if this is so but what I have said is simply the case and I don't wish to weight it in any way.

Here it is necessary to digress to give a brief account of Anglicanism and the diversity of churchmanship within it. At the time of the Reformation various reformers in different countries believed that during the Middle Ages the Church had become corrupted in some of its doctrine and life, and needed to be reformed to bring it back in line with the early Church. Reforms that led to some of the non-conformist Churches rejecting, broadly speaking, everything not explicitly attested to in the Bible. Anglicanism, which developed from the Reformation in England, adopted the position on Holy Scripture that 'whatsoever is not read therein, nor may be proved thereby, is not to be required by any man, that it should be believed as an article of faith, or be thought requisite to salvation' (Article no. 6, Articles of Religion). The Anglican Reformation retained unbroken continuity with the early Church in the essentials of the faith. These essentials are: Holy Scripture as being the rule and ultimate standard of faith, the doctrines of the historic creeds, the sacraments, distinguishing baptism and Holy Communion as having been instituted by Christ Himself and the historic orders of bishop, priest and deacon. Anglicanism was not a new Church that emerged from the Reformation but the Catholic Church reformed and retaining its essential doctrines. In Ireland Anglicanism is the Church of St Patrick reformed, while Roman Catholicism is the Church of St Patrick unreformed.

Within the same doctrinal position within Anglicanism there are broadly three interpretations or emphases. Evangelicals stress personal commitment to Jesus Christ resulting from a conversion experience. They would say that this born-again experience is a prerequisite for salvation. They emphasise the divine inspiration of scripture. High church people give importance to the authority of the Church and Anglicanism's continuity in doctrine with the early Church. They emphasise the centrality of the episcopate, the priesthood and the sacraments. Broad church is everything in between. This position objects to narrowness of definition and tends to be inclusive rather than exclusive; it contains a diversity of interpretation. Evangelicals are known as 'evans', high church people as 'spikes' and so vague and wishy-washy do these two groups consider broad church people that they don't even dignify them with a nickname. This is only a thumbnail sketch of Anglicanism and the different emphases within it and should the reader like to pursue these issues further there are volumes and volumes on these topics written by eminent theologians.

Since leaving school I had come across the YMCA version of evangelicalism. I had had a taste of it in the YMCA Cricket Club and a Sunday morning dose of it when I stayed in the YMCA hostel in Rathmines. I had also heard a public manifestation of it preached on the corner of Abbey Street and at the end of Marine Road, Dun Laoghaire. This version of Christianity did not attract me and I had never come across it in the Church of Ireland until I joined the 'Theo'. It must be said I never came across 'spikes', high-church enthusiasts either; the 'spike' is a rare bird in the Church of Ireland.

Amongst this group of ordinands the diversity of churchmanship and the differences of political allegiance and social background made for many fairly heated arguments. There were one or two who enjoyed lobbing verbal hand grenades into a peaceful group of students sitting quietly reading newspapers or books, creating consternation and taking pleasure from watching the sparks fly. I don't believe that anybody ever fell out in these arguments but there were those on all sides who were disbelieving of the views of others, both theological and political.

Most of the evangelicals came from the north and were politically Orange and Unionist and they were genuinely incredulous of the Nationalism of southerners. Some of them resented having to come to the south to study for ordination in the Church of Ireland and meeting Church of Ireland Nationalists for the first time added insult to injury. At one point a little later on there was a move by some members within the Church of Ireland in the north to have the training of ordinands shifted to Belfast, but opposition to this from level-headed members of the Church both north and south ensured that it came to nothing. This mix of north and south in the 'Theo' and later in the Divinity School was, at the end of the day, good for both. For those who were prepared to be open and listen, each learned from the other and at least moderated their often ill-informed prejudices about each other. Although people rarely changed their own positions they came to understand why others held theirs, and that was progress. The churchmanship and Orange/Green debate continued later on when in the final two years before ordination ordinands lived in the Divinity Hostel in Rathgar.

Many Divinity students at Trinity involved themselves largely if not exclusively in activities that related to their objective to be ordained. They saw their time at university as simply a means to an end. A good proportion of them read Hebrew and Oriental Languages for their degree, which was chiefly the study of the text and the world of the Old Testament and quite a few gained distinction in it. Their extra-curricular activity was Theological Society meetings when papers on theological and related subjects were read and debated. Some few prospective ordinands involved themselves in the wider activities of the university through membership of other societies and sports clubs.

After degree ordinands entered the Divinity School in Trinity and studied doctrine, church history, Bible, liturgy and ethics. They were required to live in the Divinity Hostel where they undertook pastoral and devotional training. At the Hostel there were other, mostly older, students studying a non-graduate course for ordination. This led to a touch of the oil and water problem. However there were some of the Trinity ordinands who, in my view, might have been better suited to the course that was held entirely at the Hostel and there were some taking it that should have been in Trinity.

In the Divinity School in Trinity there were two full-time professors, one full-time lecturer and a number of part-time lecturers. Just before I entered, the Regius Professor, R.R. Hartford died. Professor Vokes, Archbishop King's professor was acting Regius for a year until a replacement was appointed. Anthony and Richard Hanson, Trinity graduates and both professors of theology in English universities, were two of the Church of Ireland's most illustrious sons of modern times. The story goes that after his interview for the post of Regius Professor Vokes drove Anthony to the airport to return to England. Vokes is reputed to have told Hanson that whoever took the job would be hamstrung by the Church of Ireland bishops. When Hanson arrived home he phoned to say he was no longer interested. This was a lost opportunity for the Church of Ireland as he was a man of immense ability and a notable teacher. In 1969, at the beginning of the troubles in Northern Ireland, his twin brother Richard was appointed Bishop of Clogher. After four years he became so frustrated with Orange Protestantism, both within and outside the Church of Ireland that he resigned and returned to an academic appointment in England. He told his Diocesan Synod one year that he was shocked to find so many churches in the diocese closed during the week but he was even more shocked to find so many minds in the same condition!

Professor H.F. Woodhouse, also a Trinity graduate, teaching in British Columbia, was appointed Regius Professor of Divinity. It soon became clear to his students that although he was highly qualified academically, he was, in common with many university teachers, not an inspiring lecturer. Woodhouse's heart was in the right place; he was genuinely concerned with providing the best academic training for ordinands and he was concerned for students individually.

He retired as Regius Professor of Divinity after eighteen years and for the Church of Ireland Anthony Hanson as Regius Professor was one of the great 'might have beens.' It is possible that had he been appointed, the frustrations of coping with the pressures on the Divinity School of a conservative Church might have caused him, like his twin brother, to chuck it in after a few years and return to England.

It is possible that when Woodhouse was appointed Vokes had also applied for the job, but many within the Church of Ireland considered him too radical. As it was there had been protests to the Church authorities about his liberal attitude to biblical criticism and his questioning attitude, for example to the historicity of the Virgin Birth. In my view he presented what he called 'difficulties' in this area of study non-dogmatically, posing questions and expecting students to think them through for themselves. He saw this as his job in the context of academic freedom, but some students didn't like to have to think about things that didn't fit comfortably into their own belief systems, and upon which they had already made up their minds. Unfortunately some of his students believed that the purpose of studying the text of the Bible was to reinforce their existing prejudices the better to enable them to go out into parishes to try to replicate among their parishioners their own particular spiritual experience. In my view Vokes was not a bit too radical. His only sin was that he made aspiring clergy think, and many of them did not like it. I found that he was honest in the way he posed difficult issues. It was valuable to me since I had many questions about faith and belief and some of the doctrines of the Church. If it were not for Vokes I believe that my academic training for ordination would have been much the poorer.

It became clear early on after Woodhouse's appointment that he and Vokes were almost certainly not on each other's Christmas card list. Vokes felt he was viewed with suspicion in the Church of Ireland, so much so that he expressed surprise to a friend of mine one summer, years later, that I was prepared to entrust my parish to him to take Sunday duty for a month. Vokes' status within the university was recognised in 1976 when he was appointed Dean of the Faculty of Arts, Humanities. The board of the college must have held him in high repute in the Arts Faculty since this was a responsible office, which was by nomination of members of the faculty. When he retired after twenty-three years in the Church of Ireland he was not a Canon of either of the two Dublin Cathedrals, despite his seniority. If he had not been offered a canonry it was one thing and if he had been offered one and declined it was another, neither of which would reflect well on those in whose gift the canonries were.

Pope John XXIII opened the Second Vatican Council on 11 October 1962, and its last session was closed on 8 December 1965 by his successor Pope Paul VI. As Anglican divinity students the debates and documents of the Council were of great interest, especially the document on Ecumenism which says 'that among those Churches in which Catholic traditions and institutions in part continue to exist, the Anglican communion occupies a special place.' This was well received by ecumenical Church of Ireland divinity students but some non-ecumenical students were disdainful of it. Bishop Moorman, an official Anglican observer at the Council, pointed out that a significant proportion of the bishops of the Council came from countries like Italy and Brazil where there were virtually no Anglicans, and probably knew nothing about Anglicanism. Some of those that did know Anglicanism expressed their bafflement at the variety of theological positions within it and its apparent lack of discipline. It was therefore surprising that the Council marked Anglicanism out for special mention in this way.

After the Vatican Council the Church of Ireland Dean of Belfast, Dean Peacock, invited Bishop Moorman to speak at St Anne's Cathedral, Belfast. Paisley and his supporters mounted an aggressive protest at the Cathedral and created such trouble that the Dean cancelled the event. Paisley's bully-boy tactics won, and within the Church of Ireland the Dean's decision, while supported by some, was criticised by many as weak, and a concession to those who opposed freedom of speech. Subsequently Moorman spoke to a meeting of Church of Ireland clerics and some Divinity students in the Molesworth Hall in Dublin, where he gave an account of the Vatican Council from an Anglican point of view. A recurring theme in what he said was how the Roman Catholic Church was learning from Anglicanism. He came back to this again and again in the discussion, in what seemed to be a self-satisfied way, when a humble Divinity student raised his hand and said: 'Bishop, you keep referring to what the Roman Catholic Church has to learn from Anglicanism. What has Anglicanism to learn from Roman Catholicism?' I cannot remember what he said, but I do remember the hesitation before he answered while he adjusted his mind-set to answer the question.

Of course it was true to say that the Second Vatican Council brought about some changes that were already part of Anglicanism, e.g. the liturgy in the vernacular, the Bible for lay people and the emphasis on the Church as the people of God rather than primarily a clerical hierarchy. However, that which had the most impact on us as Church of Ireland divinity students after the Council was the flood of contacts from Catholic seminaries for the purpose, at the very least, of getting to know each other and in due course of having discussions. Since we were the only Protestant seminary in the south and there were many Catholic ones that wanted to have these events we had to limit them.

At first these occasions were purely social and slowly graduated to discussions and debates. Our numbers at the Hostel were relatively small, and there were some who were not interested in being ecumenical, so we usually met a small group in whichever Catholic seminary we went to in order not to be swamped. My memories of these occasions are the institutional atmosphere of the buildings and the seminary routine. The Catholic seminarians seemed to me to be very much subject to order and discipline, whereas in our lives there was a framework of order but we seemed to have a greater freedom in every way. I'm sure that when we entertained our Roman Catholic seminarian friends at the Hostel they found our house and routine a bit informal in comparison to their own. While we dressed casually in 'civvies' some of the Catholic seminarians still wore cassocks on their home ground, though the students who met with us tended not to. The Dominican students in Tallaght wore habits, which were a great novelty to us.

It became clear from these ecumenical exchanges that all prospective clergy, Roman Catholic and Church of Ireland, had the same hopes and aspirations for their ministries and we were all coping with the same problems. Students and clergy of our respective Churches were essentially doing the same job and coping with the same kind of issues. In my view these exchanges were an excellent development and were the basis of much good ecumenical work between the two traditions in parishes later on. Many friendships across the denominational divide were made then that still survive today. A greater understanding of each other developed and while some essential theological differences divided the two traditions these did not interfere with the development of trust and of Christian love that I believe is at the heart of the Gospel.

As a student I had the view that Church people, and especially those who were ordained, were all fine upstanding Christian people who would never say a bad word about anyone. I was naive. I discovered that amongst some clergy, and often the senior clergy at that, there was gossip, backbiting and bitchery to beat the band. It seemed to me to be more prevalent amongst some bachelor clergy for whom the Church was their whole life. Married men, while not immune, perhaps had family responsibilities to absorb their energies. In those early days I was idealistic and I was surprised at this clerical gossip but as time passed and my idealism waned I indulged in my own share of it. Talking about this to a doctor friend he assured me that the medical profession was just as bad and no doubt any other group of people sharing a common way of life. I think that people expect clergy to be morally superior to other people, and in theory maybe they should be, but in practice they are the same as everybody else. Ordination is certainly a commission to a role within the Church, but it does not transform the human nature of the ordained.

While living in the Divinity Hostel for my last two years before ordination I saw many of my fellow ordinands observing with great reverence and commitment the worship and devotional life of the chapel. Chapel was compulsory for all of us but some seemed to relish it more than others. Some of the time I found it sheer tedium. Nobody ever knows exactly what goes on in the heart of another unless the other declares it openly and even then for various reasons we cannot always rely on what people say. Our best chance of knowing what people think and believe is to observe how they behave, and some of my fellow students behaved with great devotion. We had lectures on Anglican spirituality and the devotional life of Anglican divines like Jeremy Taylor, but for me it didn't fit with my understanding of what I was about. I suppose my understanding of vocation was more practical: what some people refer to in a derogatory way as muscular Christianity. On reflection it is a matter of horses for courses.

If the sum total of the libidinal energy of all the people in the world for one day were harnessed, it would be enough to blast the earth off its axis or at least to provide heat and light for every city and town in the world for a year! Don't you love when somebody in a discussion comes out with that kind of 'fact'? Another: there are as many microbes in a square centimetre of earth as there are people in the world. We'll come to some staggering scientific facts later, but for the moment it is enough to say that I made up the first of the two above, and a friend of mine told me the other. At school science and I parted company early on so I rely entirely on others when it comes to scientific fact. Suffice to say that I made up the one about libido to make the point that it is a pretty powerful force and nobody can afford to take it for granted.

This is all a prelude to saying that by the time I came to my penultimate year before ordination I had re-met, and, as they used to say in the old days, was 'walking out' with Hilary. We had met originally at a party late on a Saturday night in a student flat in Highfield Road, Rathgar, when I was still working in insurance and sowing a few wild oats, and Hilary was working in Gouldings as a secretary. She had since left that job and had done a degree at Trinity. We re-met when she was home on holiday from teaching in England where she had gone to discover if she would like a career as a teacher before studying for a diploma in education, a requirement for teaching in Ireland, but not in England.

I'm not very good at quoting the Bible, but love comes at you 'like a thief in the night'. Love grabs hold of you to play your part in the perpetuation of the species. Marriage for Anglican ordinands is something of a complication, and one that ordinands in the Roman Catholic Church are free from, although of course this may create a different kind of problem for them. Marriage for an Anglican Divinity student complicates the practicalities of where you live and how you divide your time. Hilary and I were engaged and while the bishop who was to ordain me congratulated me warmly on my engagement he said that I could not receive the two sacraments in the same year. I must get married a year before or a year after ordination.

Having weighed everything up, Hilary and I decided that we would be married a year before I was to be ordained. This meant that in my last year in college I lived in the Divinity Hostel during term time and Hilary lived in a flat in Sandycove, and taught in Glengara Park School. Rathgar and Sandycove are only six or seven miles apart so separation was not as much of a problem for us as it was for married students from Belfast. Some older married men from the north were separated from their wives and children much of the term and went home only on occasional weekends.

6

The North

The reason there are different Christian Churches or traditions today is because in the past disagreements arose in the Church that could not be resolved and led to division. The first main division came in AD 1054 when the Eastern Orthodox Church split from the then undivided Catholic Church. The Eastern Orthodox separated over two main issues, one highly theological; the belief of the Eastern Church that the Holy Spirit proceeded from the Father only, as in the creed formulated at the Council of Nicea, and not from the Father and the Son. 'And the Son', the famous filioque clause, was interpolated into the creed at a later date and supported by the Church in Rome. The other point of irreconcilable disagreement was the use of authority in the Church by Rome.

The second main division came when different movements, mainly in the sixteenth century, led to the Churches of the Reformation splitting from the Western or Roman Church. The issues of contention were the nature of the exercise of authority over the Church by Rome, some corrupt practices, such as the sale of indulgences, and beliefs that had developed in the Church that had no warranty in Holy Scripture. The Reformation led to a number of different Churches adopting different theological emphases.

Underlying the existence of the different Christian traditions is the belief of each that they have truer knowledge or understanding of Jesus' teaching and work and of the will of God for humanity, and how most faithfully to implement this. In order to authenticate their position each tradition needs an authority for what they believe and what they teach. In broad terms the authority for Roman Catholicism is the Bible, the teachings of the Councils of the Church, tradition and the authority of the Pope. For Eastern Orthodoxy it is the Bible, the Councils of the Church before AD 1054 and tradition. For Anglicanism it is the Bible, the early Councils, tradition and reason. For some of the other Reformed Churches, the Bible and the early Councils of the Church and for some evangelical Protestants their authority is the Bible alone.

In order to copper-fasten its authority the Roman Catholic Church promulgated a doctrine at the First Vatican Council in 1870, which says that in certain defined circumstances the Pope is infallible. Anglicans say the Church is somehow infallible and some Protestant groups believe that the Bible is infallible. They all want to be infallible to prove their position is incontrovertible; if you believe you are infallible who are mere mortals or even other Christian believers to contradict you. Great stuff this infallibility. However, when everybody is infallible and all infallibly disagree, it's bound to debase the currency and lead to stalemate, and that's where we are at the moment.

This of course is all a simplification, and again there are tomes written over the centuries by theologians of all traditions in justification of the position of their own Churches. Despite the learning of theologians in this ecumenical age they haven't moved us on very far in coming to agreement on some of the main differences that divide the Churches. Power and control get in the way. The whole thing is vastly complex and it seems that lay people and some clergy are fed up to the back teeth with it and are voting with their feet and ceasing to practise religion altogether.

At one extreme of the spectrum some of the main Churches expect their rank and file members to believe the most complex and abstruse doctrines, some of which cannot be finally explained anyway. These are then designated 'a mystery', thereby in the eyes of some people giving them even more weight than if they could be understood. After all isn't life itself a mystery. People don't actually believe most of these doctrines but simply accept them on trust from their Church authorities.

At the other end of the spectrum is the little man, or maybe he is a big man or a little woman, who places him or herself strategically behind the goal in view of the cameras at sporting fixtures at Lansdowne Road and Croke Park, holding up a board saying 'John 3, 7' and reduces the whole thing to a single verse of scripture: 'Do not marvel that I say to you that you must be born again.' Whatever we may think of his text he deserves first prize for ingenuity and persistence. I'm not sure that the spectators whose view of the match he may be obscuring with his board would necessarily agree. Although I think if you watch him carefully he keeps moving, presumably in order not to antagonise people by blocking their view. How much of all this theological division and controversy, whether complex or simplistic, do you think is in pursuit of Jesus' own summary of his teaching: 'Love God and love your neighbour as yourself'? Not much, but we will come to this later.

In my pre-student days I had been to Northern Ireland only a few times, once to play cricket, once to a wedding and to an ordination selection conference. Since becoming a Divinity student I had been to Belfast on two training courses. The first was a pastoral course for which we were all allocated to parishes, given a talk by the rector and equipped with a list of his parishioners for us to visit in pairs. The parish to which I was allocated was in a working class area close to the shipyards. When we called we were usually warmly received and mothered by the woman of the house; the men were almost invariably out. That my partner and I were both from the south was a topic of conversation and we were regaled with the names and track record of clergy from the south they had known. The abiding memory I have is the warmth with which these women received us in their tiny kitchen houses. They had an attitude towards us of 'God love you aren't you lovely young men', as they would say, 'going for the Church'. This expression always conjures up in my mind a picture of a divinity student bent forward, thumbs to each temple, index fingers forward simulating horns and like a bull, charging at the side wall of a church!

We also went on a tour of a biscuit factory on the Newtownards Road, conducted by a manager proud as punch of his factory and determined to tell us every last detail about it. The workers, mainly women in overalls, their hair tied up in white muslin, talked to each other while they worked and shared jokes about this troupe of earnest young men listening intently to the boss, and mystified at what could be interesting about what, to them, was their daily tedium.

For the third component of the course a Canon Craig gave us a talk about conducting the liturgy. His emphasis was the Anglican principle of worship; everything to be done 'decently and in order'. The only thing I remember in particular of what he said was that when conducting a service we should always have a clean, ironed handkerchief and keep it up a sleeve so that we didn't have to root through the cassock opening to draw it out from our trouser pocket. Lay people may not realise that there is a way through the cassock to the trousers to facilitate rooting in this way, though it always looks inelegant. Gilbert Wilson, later Bishop, now dead, in the days when visual aids were in fashion, once stood on the chancel steps at a children's service to talk to the children. When everybody had sat down he started to root through his cassock into his trousers' pockets, first one side then the other. Then he announced to the children that he could not tell them the story he had prepared for them because he couldn't find his balls. Such inelegant rooting before a church full of children, mothers in their best hats and fathers in their Sunday suits is entirely un-Anglican!

The second training course we attended in Belfast was at Purdysburn Psychiatric Hospital, the largest psychiatric hospital in Northern Ireland. We lived in student quarters for the best part of a week. We were allocated in pairs to consultants in order that they introduce us to the whole area of mental illness. A friend and I were placed with Dr Lyons, a senior psychiatrist who later conducted significant research into the psychiatric effects of the troubles in Northern Ireland, and his registrar Dr Potter. We were lucky; they were both excellent teachers and took a good deal of trouble to plan a programme for us. They set a timetable for the week designed to teach us as much as possible in a practical way, such that it would be of most use to us in our role as clergy in parishes.

We spent one whole morning sitting in while Dr Lyons conducted consultations with patients whom he had selected to cover a broad spectrum of common psychiatric illnesses. When each came in he introduced the patient to us as students and asked their permission for us to be present. He then asked them how they were and about their progress. When they left he would ask us what we thought was the problem. Sometimes it was obvious, as in the case of depression, and sometimes it wasn't. He would then tell us what the particular illness was and how to identify it if we came across it in a parishioner, what best to do if it had not been diagnosed and how best to be supportive if it had.

He brought in one man in his late sixties, small, comfortable, corduroys and hands in the pockets of his woolly cardigan. He smiled and chatted away to us in a friendly way; anybody's favourite uncle.

'Not much wrong with this one, what's he doing here?' I thought to myself, as Dr Lyons asked him questions that without background information were of no help to us in identifying his illness. After he left Dr Lyons asked us: 'Well, what do you think?' Neither of us could come up with anything.

'That old boy's a flasher. Good job, family reared, and he's still exposing himself. He has been to prison in the past and he's in here by order of the court.' Then Dr Lyons explained the illness, probable causes and treatment.

One patient was suffering from schizophrenia, another from manic depression, a young man of about eighteen was homosexual and another an alcoholic. This was 1965 when aversion therapy was still used for young homosexuals in the hope of curing what was described as their deviant sexual urge. They were shown erotic homosexual films and when they became aroused an electric shock was applied to their genitals. Even at that early stage of my understanding I considered this barbaric and said something to this effect. Dr Lyons conceded that the treatment did not have much success.

Aversion therapy for alcoholics was administered by putting a couple of patients into a simulated bar, created in a room in the hospital, with counter, bottles, beer mats, advertisements and all the other appurtenances of a normal bar. The patients were locked in and allowed to choose whatever they wanted to drink, and when they started drinking they were given an antibooze tablet, which by its reaction with the alcohol made them violently sick. The patient would have another drink and the same again. They were left in the simulated bar for a long period in foul conditions. They saw each other vomiting and their vomit was not cleaned up. The smell of booze, getting repeatedly violently ill and generally being allowed to degenerate into a terrible state was supposed to create in the patient an aversion to alcohol. I understand that both of these aversion therapies have long since been abandoned. I did, however, learn a great deal on this course that was useful to me over the years.

I was ordained in June 1967 and went as curate to the parish of St John Orangefield, on Castlereagh Road, Belfast. To a southerner, Belfast was noticeably different from Dublin. The buses and letterboxes were red, the police carried guns, suburban houses were generally of different design and finish, and even the tarmacadam of the roads had a different hue. The flag on public buildings was the union jack and virtually everything closed on Sundays including children's playgrounds where the swings were chained up on the orders of Protestant controlled local authorities to prevent children desecrating the Lord's Day.

In Belfast you had the Roman Catholic Church, the Presbyterian Church, the Church of Ireland, the Methodist Church, no doubt a small Orthodox community and, somebody calculated, as many as fifty other Protestant denominations, gospel halls and sects. Working in a Church of Ireland parish I met exclusively Protestants, any one of whom in those days would have choked on his/her scrambled egg at the thought that in thirty-five years time a member of Sinn Féin would be elected Lord Mayor of Belfast. They might have recovered somewhat, but they would have been incredulous that he would place a wreath on the war memorial in Donegall Square in commemoration of Ulstermen that had died at the Somme.

Having been brought up in the south of Ireland and especially coming from a liberal family, I had a number of Catholic friends and was perfectly comfortable living in a Catholic society where the Protestant minority was fairly evenly dispersed throughout the community. In Northern Ireland people, largely speaking, live either in Catholic or Protestant areas. When I went to Belfast after ordination, as a Church of Ireland curate, naturally I lived in a Protestant area. Strangely enough it took me a while to pick up on the fact that no Roman Catholics that I knew of lived nearby. In three years in Belfast, Hilary and I met only one Catholic that we knew of. No doubt we dealt with Catholics in shops and offices and we saw from time to time a Catholic friend from the south, but we met only one indigenous Catholic in our time in Belfast and he was a friend of a friend.

Discrimination against Catholics was institutionalised in the political process of Northern Ireland and the Stormont system of 'democracy' rendered Nationalist politicians virtually powerless. The most flagrant discrimination was in the area of housing, and particularly in Derry. The housing issue was used effectively to gerrymander constituencies to the advantage of Unionists. Catholics had a great deal of genuine grievance. In 1963 Lord Brookborough had resigned as prime minister of Northern Ireland. He had boasted that he hadn't got a Roman Catholic 'about the place', and considered all Catholic's as potential traitors. He refused on more than one occasion the friendly overtures of the Taoiseach, Seán Lemass.

Terence O'Neill, shortly after he was appointed Brookborough's successor, stated as one of his objectives: '... to build bridges between the two traditions within our community', and two years later he invited Lemass to visit Stormont. When Hilary and I went to live in Belfast there was still great hope amongst moderate people on both sides of the community that injustice might be rooted out and that trust and confidence might be built up between the two communities. However, extremist Protestant/Unionist reaction to O'Neill and his policies had already begun with demonstrations, often violent, many of them led by Paisley. In the new atmosphere Nationalists marched in pursuance of civil rights in the manner of Martin Luther King and the civil rights marches of the United States.

By 1969 the Civil Rights Association was active and marching peacefully in pursuit of their objectives. These marches were vigorously and sometimes violently opposed by Loyalists in the tradition of 'Croppy lie down.' A civil rights march from Belfast to Derry composed mainly of People's Democracy students of Queens University was harassed on its route and violently attacked by supporters of Paisley at Burntollet Bridge where serious injuries were inflicted on the marchers. As far as some loyalists were concerned Nationalists, and for Nationalist read 'Catholic,' had no rights and should be thankful for all the benefits they enjoyed living in Northern Ireland. If they didn't like it they should pack up and move to the Republic and, as they saw it, live in poverty under the heel of the Roman Catholic Church.

The IRA seized its opportunity and taking advantage of the disturbances provoked by loyalist reaction to civil rights marches perpetrated its terrorist campaign. This in turn led to counter terrorism from loyalist paramilitaries. After thirty years of violence by paramilitaries on both sides and the armed forces response by the civil authority, little was achieved. 3,000 people were killed, thousands maimed and there was widespread destruction of property. There was untold grief, hurt and heartache for thousands of families.

During these thirty years brave heroic IRA snipers positioned themselves at upstairs windows and shot policemen in the street below. These policemen were guilty of nothing but doing their job. Equally brave and heroic Protestant paramilitaries walked into pubs frequented by Catholics and sprayed unarmed civilians with gunfire, killing innocent people, old and young, men and women alike, simply because they were Catholics. Tit-for-tat killings of ordinary citizens took place in local areas for no other reason than that the victims were Catholic or Protestant.

After all this hatred, after all the cowardly violence, after all the death and destruction, after the polarisation of both communities, both sides eventually had to sit down and come to a political solution. Some Protestants believe that this solution has reversed the situation of thirty years ago and discriminates against them and in favour of Catholics. Of course there were rights and wrongs on both sides, in different proportions at different times and in different situations. All we can do is hope that whatever imbalance there still is will be resolved without a return to violence.

What is most significant in reflecting on all of this is that undergirding the position of both sides is religion; the Roman Catholicism of Nationalists and the Protestantism of Unionists. Both religions believe in Jesus Christ as their Lord and Master. This Jesus whom they acknowledge as God, himself summed up his teaching as 'Love God and love your neighbour as yourself'. He taught explicitly and unequivocally 'love your enemies, do good to those who hate you, bless those who curse you, pray for those who abuse you and turn the other cheek.'

How could faithful members of both religions, when these commands are central to the teaching of Jesus, perpetrate virulent hatred against each other? The fact is that most people on both sides simply ignore these commands of Jesus. They choose not to take account of them. It seems that they suspend any commitment to love and forgiveness when dealing with members of the other Christian tradition. On the face of it, it seems that people on both sides believe that they should judge, condemn and hate the other because they belong to a Church that holds different abstract theological doctrines from their own. These differences of doctrine are in the areas of understanding the eucharist, the authority and infallibility of the Pope, the authority and infallibility of the Bible, justification by faith alone and many more.

People ignore the simple, practical, clear and easily understood teachings of Jesus on love and forgiveness and claim to base their hatred on different theological issues that were central to the Reformation four hundred years in the past. Roman Catholicism says that Protestants go to hell and some Protestants say that Roman Catholics go to hell, so is it any wonder that other people say that, as far as they are concerned, they can all go to hell and don't go near church, chapel or meeting house?

In Northern Ireland, however, these non-practising Christians, agnostics or atheists are either Catholic or Protestant non-practising Christians, agnostics or atheists and hold the same antagonisms to the other side as religious people. This suggests that each behaves with bitterness and hatred against the other, not on Christian grounds but on tribal grounds and their behaviour is entirely contrary to the Gospel of Jesus Christ.

It seems that over the centuries doctrinal conformity was the criterion by which, to put it mildly, the Churches counted people in or out. Christian love had no place in how orthodoxy dealt with doctrinal deviancy or division. In mediaeval times doctrinal difference was enough to justify cutting out tongues, gouging out eyes and torturing and burning people at the stake. These appalling atrocities were committed by the Church, or by civil authorities with the support or on behalf of the Church. In Northern Ireland in modern times Christian love had no place when hatred and bitterness caused people of different religious traditions to burn people out of their homes, maim and murder each other. I suppose we have moved on in that the Churches as institutions did not perpetrate these modern day atrocities. Individuals who claimed allegiance to one Church or the other perpetrated them.

Is it naive to suggest that things in Northern Ireland could have been different? What if the Churches had preached and indoctrinated their members as effectively with Christian love and forgiveness as they did with abstract doctrinal differences and tribal allegiance? How could the love of God and of neighbour which Jesus laid on his followers as the central requirement of their discipleship, have been virtually ignored by the institutional Churches in their attitude to their fellow Christians who differed in doctrine?

In the past in Northern Ireland Churches held entrenched positions. There was a stand-off by which there was little contact between the Churches or their clergy. From time to time there were issues of contention and controversy between them. The whole attitude of each to the other caused Catholics and Protestants to have as little contact as possible. There was suspicion, not trust, and in the extreme, mutual antagonism leading to hatred, civil strife and murder. I believe the clergy on both sides, largely speaking over the years, did not actively promote hatred that led to violence, but they didn't do much to stop it either. Did Protestant clergy preach love of Catholics or did Catholic clergy preach love of Protestants? I don't believe they did. In the parable of the good Samaritan Jesus said, 'the Jews had no dealings with the Samaritans.' Can there be a parable more appropriate to Northern Ireland? Perhaps some clergy did preach it and apply it to the other side, but if they did they didn't get much of a hearing. It is still hard to accept that when love is the centre of the Christian gospel so many people who call themselves Christian, both Catholic and Protestant, hate each other.

Hatred between religions, as we know, is not unique to Northern Ireland or to different kinds of Christianity. Sunni and Shiite Muslims are often bitterly opposed and there is a group that claims to be Islamic, the Ahmadi, that other branches of Islam say is not Muslim at all. They are proscribed by law and persecuted in Pakistan. Some Hindus and Muslims hate and murder each other in the name of their religions. Jews and Arabs, generally speaking, are not in love with each other. In the history of humankind religion has been more a curse than a blessing. However the whole thing, it seems, is not as simple as it sounds, and has more to do with land and power and control than appears on the surface. Desmond Tutu said: 'When the white man came to Africa he had the Bible and we had the land. The white man said "let us pray", and when we opened our eyes we had the Bible and he had the land.'

St John's Parish was a lower middle-class parish in the south east of the city. Hilary and I were well received by parishioners, and Hilary developed an interest of her own with the Marriage Counselling Service. I worked hard in the parish, at last doing what I had worked for for six years. I worked all the hours of the day and took Monday as my day off. We normally drove down to Dublin on Sunday night after Evening Prayer and back again early on Tuesday morning in time for the weekly staff meeting with the rector, when he shared out between us the duties for the week.

I have no way of knowing if it is true of Catholic churchgoers, but there is a particularly respectable and sometimes puritan air about Protestant ones. They project a butter-wouldn't-melt-in-the-mouth image, especially to the clergy. However, you are not in a parish long before you see human nature breaking through, sometimes by chance. I once bumped into two regular churchgoers, one married to somebody else, holding hands in the church grounds. Sometimes in the privacy of their own homes people tell you the most surprising things that, knowing the person from going to church, you would never suspect in a hundred years. This is the basis on which non-churchgoers level the accusation of hypocrisy against churchgoers, and often with some justification. However non-churchgoers may not be entirely free of that particular disorder themselves.

Drinking alcohol, as a general rule, would have been suspect, if not considered out of court, to many parishioners. One notable exception to my knowledge was the choir who, as far as drinking was concerned, were a pretty normal group of people. The dynamics of church choirs, where relationships are not always what they seem, would make an interesting behavioural study. The pursuit of good church music, which the choir is there to lead, does not always square with the ideal of Christian worship.

One evening I arrived home at about 9.30 pm, and felt like going out for a drink after a long hard day, so Hilary and I went to 'The Rosetta', a few streets away. We went upstairs to the lounge bar, sat down and ordered a drink. Looking around the bar I saw four members of the choir relaxing after choir practice. One of them turned and caught my eye and her body language screamed embarrassment. She half smiled and then bent forward and said something to the others which was clearly along the lines: 'Don't look now, but the new curate and his wife are over there.' We made it our business not to look in their direction again, and when we finished our drink we waved across as we left. I had no difficulty with them seeing me in a pub, but I know they were embarrassed that I had seen them.

Next time we went out for a drink we went to a pub up the hills well out of the parish and walked straight into a member of the youth club committee who chatted away normally to us and wasn't the slightest bit embarrassed. On a day off down the Ards peninsula Hilary and I went into a pub for lunch and I just caught sight of a woman, a parishioner making for the door with her male companion. She had seen me first. For some people whatever you're up to, it's a case of don't let the clergy know.

I'm not sure why clergy have only one day off a week while most other people have two, especially when clergy, much of the time, work three periods of the day while most 'ordinary' people work only two. But then clergy don't work to earn their living; they have a vocation and they are not paid a wage or salary, they are paid a stipend in order to free them from the necessity of earning their living, in order to pursue their vocation.

My work in St John's was mostly with the youth club and with the sick and the housebound. Some of the old people were marvellous and despite infirmities of one kind or another they were glad to be as well as they were and appreciated a visit from the clergy. Tea drinking became an occupational hazard and after an afternoon's visiting one floated home and never wanted to see a cup of tea again. There was one exception amongst the old; a woman who lived on her own and always produced a nip of whiskey, and I don't believe she drank herself. Maybe she did; perhaps she was a secret drinker, but she poured one for me and she didn't have one. She was from Dublin.

The only crematorium in Ireland at the time was in the parish and the rector of St John's was the Church of Ireland chaplain. They burned only Protestants because the Roman Catholic Church forbade cremation at the time. When the rector was on holiday or not available I took chaplaincy duty at the crematorium. This meant conducting the service in the chapel when the remains had been brought a distance and the local clergy hadn't travelled. Many of these funerals came from the Republic, where as yet there was no crematorium.

Since the funerals I took normally came from the country or the south, their arrival time at the crematorium was an estimate, and since 'never be late for a funeral' was an important principle for clergy, I often spent time while I waited, talking to one of the attendants. One was a particularly affable elderly gentleman, a Mr Johnston, who told me he was a Presbyterian, but there was one thing he admired about the Church of Ireland: 'When a Presbyterian funeral comes in here,' he said, 'if the deceased is a widow from a kitchen house on the Newtownards Road they could be in and out in ten minutes. If the deceased is an important person from the Malone Road they might be in there for the best part of an hour. With the Church of Ireland they all get the same treatment.'

I wasn't entirely sure that this was so, for while death is indeed 'the leveller', human nature will try to mask this truth to the very end. Only recently, I saw a funeral notice in the paper for a member of the aristocracy stipulating 'Morning Dress' – the poor foolish people! A certain clergyman I know, who had only recently been ordained, was taking his first funeral. After the service of reception the widow called him over to the coffin and pointed out that of nine words on the breastplate five had been mis-spelled. This was not good enough. Her husband was not going to his grave with five mis-spellings on his coffin. Next day when the hearse arrived at the cemetery the mourners were asked to wait while the hearse detoured behind some trees, where an undertaker's man whipped off the breastplate and replaced it with another. The hearse re-joined the mourners and the man was lowered into his grave with every last word on his breastplate spelled correctly.

One day Mr Johnston at the crematorium asked me if, after I had finished the service, I would like to see 'downstairs'. With some misgivings I agreed since I felt he wanted to show me around. He showed me an oven that I'm glad to say was not in use at the time and explained how with the intense heat the coffin burned immediately and the wood ash was fanned off and disposed of. Since approximately 80 per cent of the human body is water all that was left after the whole process was ash from the bones and these, for the average person weighed about three pounds. In a little side room there were metal boxes with sliding lids and a name and the person's religious denomination on each. These contained the ashes of people that had not been claimed by their families.

When a certain length of time had passed the chaplain of the particular denomination performed an interment service for unclaimed ashes in the lawn of the crematorium. There might be six or eight boxes on the grass in a row with a sod of turf turned back beside each. After prayers of committal an attendant would pour the ashes into the earth and replace the sod; an anonymous end to lives that had begun no doubt with great joy for their families. These were people who had loved and been loved, and there was nobody of their own present to mark their return to the earth.

On the political front in Northern Ireland at this time the Prime Minister, Terence O'Neill, acknowledged the need for reform in response to the Civil Rights campaign, and began to move in that direction. After Burntollet it became evident that militant elements had taken over the Civil Rights Association and its activity became confrontation and provocation rather than protest. In early 1969 an explosion destroyed an electricity substation at Castlereagh, a couple of miles up the road from where we lived. A few weeks later over a period of a week three mains water pipelines were sabotaged and an electricity pylon was destroyed. The police attributed these acts of terrorism to Republicans. Later it transpired that the sabotage had been the work of Loyalists with the intention of Republicans being blamed, in order to exert pressure on O'Neill to put a stop to reform or even to resign. The ruse worked. Shortly afterwards O'Neill resigned and was succeeded by his cousin Major James Chichester Clark, who committed himself to continuing with reforms.

During the summer there were serious riots in West Belfast and on 12 July there was fierce street violence in Belfast and Derry. All of this culminated in August in the Battle of the Bogside in Derry. Rioting and shootings throughout Northern Ireland, particularly in the Falls/Shankill area of Belfast, followed. By the end of August ten people had been killed, and many areas of Belfast were war zones.

Living in a peaceful area of the city, the worst Hilary and I experienced was to be woken at nights by the army putting up roadblocks on the road outside. The nearest street violence to St John's was on the Newtownards Road, where local clergy from surrounding parishes did what they could at night-time to calm people on the streets. This often meant staying out until the small hours of the morning until everyone had gone home. The Salvation Army was there too, providing tea and comfort for frightened and weary people. They are a Christian body with a facility for being on the spot where there is human need.

A large number of RUC officers lived in the parish and there was a deep sense of shock when Constable Arbuckle, the first RUC casualty of the troubles, was killed in October 1969. I have a clear memory of his funeral passing our house on Castlereagh Road on its way to Roselawn Cemetery. A police band played the dead march and RUC top brass and a rank of officers walked behind. In the despondency of the time, little could people have imagined that 300 RUC officers would be killed over the next thirty years.

Though I never advertised the fact, I was known in the parish to be southern, Nationalist and ecumenical. During all this period nobody ever said anything to me, despite the fact that I could not bring myself to sing 'God Save the Queen' on Armistice Sunday, and stood mute in view of a full church.

I had always intended to stay in Belfast for no more than three years and by this time I had plans in train to spend a year studying at the Divinity School of the University of Chicago, with the compliments of the World Council of Churches. So in August 1970 Hilary and I set sail for America.

7

America

When we told people we were going to Chicago the most frequent response we received was some reference to gangsters. The image that people had of the city where we were to live for the next year came from the era of Al Capone; illicit booze, gang warfare, and the St Valentine's Day Massacre. As it transpired Al Capone's brother lived in benign retirement a few blocks away from our student apartment in Hyde Park, in the university area. This was the only association between the Chicago we knew and the days, long past, of prohibition and associated gangland murders.

There was, however, another 'gangster' operating in Chicago during our time there; Richard J. Daley, who had been mayor since 1955. He ran the city Tamany Hall style, using a political machine, the tentacles of which reached into every corner of Chicago life. He was in the tradition of American city bosses of earlier days and he kept control by widespread job patronage, from street cleaners to judges. Reading the Chicago newspapers and talking to people one had a sense of the grip that Daley and his machine had on the city. Daley or the Democrats, who were one and the same thing, were constantly challenged on this, that or the other corruption. Daley, with a knack for conceding acceptable human failings, managed to stay beyond the taint of corruption, but some of his associates did not. Shortly after we arrived in Chicago, Paul Powell, the Secretary of State for Illinois, though officially outside Daley's immediate sphere of influence, died suddenly, allegedly in bed with his mistress. The police found $800,000 in banknotes in shoeboxes in his apartment; money believed to be bribes to do with the issue of trucking licences.

Towards the end of our time in Chicago Daley stood for yet another term as mayor. Jesse Jackson, was just becoming known through his work as director of Operation Breadbasket in Chicago, an economic arm of Martin Luther King's southern Christian Leadership Conference. He challenged in the courts a law that made it virtually impossible for an independent to receive enough signatures for nomination to run for mayor. He lost his case and this left two candidates, Daley and a Republican, Benjamin Adamowski. To date in the twentieth century There had never been more than two candidates in a mayoral election. Daley was re-elected with 66 per cent of the vote. Most of the faculty at the University would have supported Adamowski, despite the fact that they knew if he were elected, because of his inexperience, there was a danger of chaos in the city, but they could not bring themselves to support Daley. One faculty member, however, told me she would vote for Daley on the grounds that despite his corrupt regime, he made the city function efficiently. All of this was before there was political corruption in Ireland!

While Daley would often speak the truth, on the face of it, there was usually a twist. In one sweltering summer when many cities around America turned on the fire hydrants to allow children in the black ghettos and poor areas to cool down, Daley said: 'Not in Chicago. We'll provide our children with swimming pools,' and he did. But he put in pools approximately the same size as many families in the suburbs had in their back gardens to cater for the hundreds of children in the black ghettos. In 1968, two years before we went to Chicago there had been the infamous episode when police brutally beat protesters outside the Democratic National Convention that met in the city to elect a Democratic candidate for the presidency to succeed Lyndon B. Johnston. It is believed, and not without reason, that orders to the police came directly from the mayor.

Before he left office Johnston had scaled down the bombing of North Vietnam and had stated his intention of seeking peace talks. Nixon, his successor, continued to scale back operations but the war continued. In May 1970, three months before we arrived in America, the Ohio National Guard shot dead four students at a campus anti-war protest at Kent State University. This resulted in widespread serious disorder on university campuses across America. Some of my fellow students, now in Chicago as postgraduates, had been involved in these disturbances and all of them were still angry about Kent State. Many of them had become radical and vociferous anti-war campaigners because of it.

The Divinity School of the University of Chicago was a prestigious postgraduate school. There was a number of older students like myself; clergy and sisters of main line denominations, and some clergy who belonged to American denominations I had never heard of. Most of the students I took courses with were straight from college; bright young Americans, many of them interested in studying theology for its own sake. Some came from non-churchgoing families and were themselves not churchgoers, while one or two planned to be ordained. For me it was refreshing to study with these people and they in turn were interested, and sometimes slightly amused, by my accounts of life in the conservative Church of Ireland.

Hilary quickly found a good secretarial job at the University Hospital, but we had to make 'adjustments' in order not to be considered old fogies by my young fellow students. One of them, Felix, of Latin American origin, had long black hair and an unkempt beard and looked like pictures of Jesus Christ, about whom in fact he didn't know a great deal. Because of his appearance he was constantly being stopped by the police and searched for drugs. When they didn't find any, since he didn't use them, they hassled him on the grounds that his appearance suggested he did. He was a delightfully gentle soul who didn't deserve the harassment the police gave him.

Scott Ledaney came from a wealthy family. His father owned a wiener, or hot dog sausage, factory. He was often taken for Irish as Scott Delaney. He knew he would end up running the family business, but in the meantime he wanted to discover what all this religion was about and if there was something more important in life than making wieners. Early on he invited me for a meal to ask me about what I believed and how I saw my work as a clergyman. He was fascinated to hear my story and to learn about religion in Ireland.

Mary B Good who had been brought up a Protestant and had recently converted to Catholicism was one of the few churchgoers in the group. She was active, particularly in adult education, in her local parish. She was a kind and gentle young woman, committed, but she displayed none of the excesses of the zeal of the newly converted. Despite her own recent spiritual journey she was open and interested in other people's experiences. By the end of the first term she and Bill, whose background I didn't know, had fallen in love and were living together. All of the others in the group knew but they hid it for some time from Hilary and me lest we be shocked, which gives an idea of the kind of image they had of us.

Around this time T-groups, that is groups exploring the workings of group dynamics, were coming on the scene. Between Christmas and Easter Hilary and I took part with my fellow students in an extra-curricular T-group that was conducted by a senior member of the Divinity faculty, Professor Charles Stinette, and met one night a week. All went fairly smoothly until about the third night when one of the group flew at Hilary and me: 'What's all this Professor and Dr Stinette. Why don't you call him by his name?' Mary came in quickly to soften the challenge and asked gently: 'Pat and Hilary, why don't you call him Chuck like the rest of us?' We explained that where we came from such informality by students with a senior member of the faculty, twice our age, was not acceptable and although there might be a chance we would call him Charles, Chuck would definitely stick in our throats! Chuck, Charles, Professor Stinette remained silent and continued to make notes through all the ensuing discussion on the diversity of cultural backgrounds within the group. We learned a few years after we came home from Chicago that Mary B. Good and Bill had married. They had one son and in her early thirties Mary died of cancer.

Mel was an Afro-American who had worked in the nearby black ghetto as a youth leader. He and his wife Judy and two small children lived in an apartment and had to pay a rent loaded by over 50 per cent because they were black and the insurance on their Volkswagen beetle was loaded for the same reason. One Saturday Mel brought Hilary and me into the black ghetto that surrounded the University on three sides, just to see what life was like for most Afro-Americans. We could never have gone there on our own but Mel was so well known and liked through his youth work and was greeted so warmly by people, we felt entirely at ease. Housing conditions were like Gardiner Street, Dublin in the 1950s: different kinds of houses, but the same overcrowding and social deprivation. There was an atmosphere of hopelessness with fine able-bodied men ambling around aimlessly or sitting on steps in front of houses minding children. We saw one of the tiny swimming pools that Daley provided to show America that Chicago children didn't need to use fire hydrants to keep cool in hot summers. When we told some of our other student friends, all Americans, where we had been they conceded that none of them had ever been into a black ghetto.

The husband of one of the group, himself not a student, was a conscientious objector, and in lieu of service in Vietnam, he did community service as a porter at the University Hospital. He was an accomplished pianist and hoped to become a concert performer. The status of conscientious objector was not easy to attain. An applicant could not just have a recent conversion to pacifism but had to show through a rigorous investigation that their value system in the past included pacifism in some shape or form. For the others their student status postponed the draft and by the time most of them finished at university the end of the war was in sight.

One of the Divinity School library assistants was an unlikely American. He didn't drive. Tom was short, stoutish and wore sandals. He was what Americans call a PK – a preacher's kid; his father had been a minister in a non-conformist church. When he left school he joined the army and for a time was a cryptographer at US army headquarters in Tokyo. After the army he did a degree in English literature and in 1959 came to Chicago.

Tom was an only child, his parents were dead and he was alone in the world. He was by conversion a convinced, but only occasionally practising, Anglican. He was not particularly religious but he loved the high Anglican liturgy of the Episcopal Church on campus, and attended it some Sundays; he believed that it did not behove a proper Anglican to indulge in excess. He was, as he said himself, a loyal American and an Anglophile, an essential part of which was his Anglicanism. Politically he claimed to be a monarchist, but of course a constitutional one. He was of unfailing good humour, had a sharp wit and used both to mitigate the monotony of handing out books to students all day.

When he first discovered where I was from and what I did, his response was: 'My God, I don't believe it, an Irish Anglican. I knew they existed but I didn't think I'd ever meet one,' and for the next couple of weeks he introduced me to all and sundry, like a circus freak, as 'an Irish Anglican priest.' Tom read novels in French and when he came to Europe on holiday always visited England and France. Over the years he came to stay with us, having established before his first visit that, as an Anglophile, he would be safe in Ireland! He came, he said, to pursue his Irish education.

There were some well-known and interesting people on the faculty of the Divinity School. Paul Tillich had held a professorship for the last three years of his life and died there in 1965. Paul Ricoeur, the French Protestant philosopher/theologian, was there during my time and gave occasional public lectures. Martin E. Marty, a Missouri Conference Lutheran theologian, well known in America, travelled so much he lived half way between O'Hare airport and the University, and posted his weekly schedule on a notice board in his kitchen that included slots for quality time with each of his children. His great fear in life was that if he inadvertently ingested the skin of a nut kernel he had minutes to get to a hospital or he might die. It had happened a couple of times and I believe he still survives.

The most interesting faculty member I came to know was the New Testament scholar, R.M. Grant. In the Divinity School in Trinity we had used his 'Introduction to the New Testament'. He told me that since writing that book he had moved his area of interest to the early Church as there was nothing more of significance to be said about the New Testament until there was new source material and there was none he knew of in the offing. What was needed was something like a New Testament equivalent of the Dead Sea Scrolls, the name given to the remains of a collection of Hebrew and Aramaic manuscripts discovered in 1947 near the Dead Sea by chance, by a shepherd in the desert looking, appropriately, for a lost sheep. I remember confronting myself with the proposition that God might further authenticate his momentous and unique revelation of himself to the world, in Jesus Christ, by something like the chance discovery of scrolls in a desert cave. As Ronald Knox said, 'How odd of God to choose the Jews,' but also 'How strange a way to have His say.'

R.M. Grant was an Anglican priest and on Sundays he took part in the liturgy in the local Episcopal Church. He was reputed to have made a lot of money dealing in stocks and shares. He used to recount the story of a bishop of the early church in Egypt who had a sideline as a banker, and he wondered what modern day bishops did with their spare time! His other great interest was First World War German U-boats. He was an authority on the subject and had published extensively on it. I put him in touch with John de Courcy Ireland, the Irish naval historian, who was able to tell him that a U-boat wreck had been discovered when the Irish Naval Service was searching for the Aer Lingus plane that crashed in the vicinity of Tuskar Rock. Dr de Courcy Ireland, thanks to one of R.M. Grant's books, had been able to tell a surviving German U-boat captain, Captain Weisbach of *U 19*, with whom he was friendly, the fate of his brother who had been lost in another U-boat, *U 74*. Until then Capt. Weisbach had never been exactly informed of his brother's fate.

From time to time interesting people visited the university. Richard Murphy, the Irish poet, gave a reading and was well received. Anthony Wedgwood-Benn who had been a Minister in the Labour government that had recently left office, gave a public lecture on the current political situation in the UK. At a question and answer session after the lecture I asked him about the British government's responsibility for violence in Northern Ireland. To my surprise he would not address the question, abruptly giving the stock British government line of the time: 'That's a matter for Stormont.'

Hilary and I lived in foreign married student accommodation provided by the University. Derrick and Joan, an English couple, were in the same apartment building. Derrick was spending a year in the law school and Joan, a nurse, worked at the hospital. We became friendly and did things together. Despite emergency telephones on every street corner and tight security, robberies and violence were commonplace on the campus. One night we four were at a party in the apartment of a New Zealand couple five or six blocks away. At about one in the morning we started phoning for a taxi and couldn't get one. In the end there was nothing for it, despite the risk, but to walk. We left our watches, wallets and jewellery behind and each took a five-dollar bill in case we were robbed. If an assailant got some money he was less likely to assault you. We linked arms and set out nervously humming a tune quietly to relieve tension, and suddenly we would cross the street in case we were followed. We got home safely but we were determined not to be out on foot in Hyde Park at night again. We understood why some people who worked with Hilary suggested that she might consider carrying a gun in her handbag.

On Friday or Saturday evenings in particular we would get together in the apartment of either of us, often with Alain and Regine and sometimes with Hartmut and Karine, French and German couples who also lived in the same apartment building. Alain and Hartmut were both at the law school with Derrick. We made our own fun and consumed moderate quantities of Californian wine and Budweiser beer.

Hartmut was about thirty and completing his third doctorate. Karine was a judge at home in Germany where there is a professional judiciary. They had a baby son. Hartmut spoke English perfectly and Alain told us he spoke French with no discernible accent. One warm Saturday evening on our way to one of the quads to listen to a band, Hilary and I met Hartmut, Karine and the baby on their way back from the lake. We weren't long at the quad when Hartmut arrived beside us: 'Is Karine not with you?' Hilary asked.

'No,' he replied, 'she's putting the baby to bed. She wanted him so she has to look after him,' and she was getting the meal too.

One night after dinner in their apartment Hartmut cornered me and wanted to talk about Ireland. He told me all about his great interest in Celtic civilisation. The same Hartmut wasn't inclined to ask questions. He told me that one day he planned to go to Ireland to pursue his interest. Then he suddenly said: 'You Irish have a great sense of humour. That's my next project; to develop my sense of humour.'

I thought he was joking, but he wasn't, and he proceeded to tell me some puerile jokes and asked me what I thought.

One evening Derrick asked me if I would go to the law courts in downtown Chicago the following day with him; he wanted to see an American court in operation. We arrived at the court building, went into the first court we came to, passed the armed policeman and tip-toed quietly into the public seats at the back. It was a large court with an Afro-American female judge on the bench. The court was full and the judge was having a barney with a lawyer at the front. When that case was over she looked straight down in our direction and said at the top of her voice: 'Who are you?'

Derrick rose tentatively.

'Yes, you two. Stand up' she said in a garrulous way. We stood up.

'We're law students from the University of Chicago,' Derrick replied.

'What are you doing here?'

'We've come to see the workings of an American court.'

'Where are you from?'

'England.' Derrick said to keep it simple.

'Come up here.' We pushed our way along the public gallery, out into the aisle and went up to the front, not knowing what to expect.

'Sit there,' the judge said, pointing to a compartment to the right and just in front of her on the elevated bench facing down the court. She then proceeded to hear the next case. As I sat there I dreaded the thought of what she might say if I had to declare that not only was I a clergyman, but that I was not from England. When the case finished she looked over and still at the top of her voice said to us: 'Well, what do you think?' Derrick smiled and said something non-committal.

'Now go back to England,' she said, 'and tell them how well we administer justice in Chicago.' We smiled and thanked her, and made our way down the court and out onto the street, glad to be there. We learned later that we had landed by chance in the court of a well-known character of Chicago's judiciary and a Daley appointee.

In Ireland we are familiar with what St Patrick's Day means in American cities and how they celebrate it. On 17 March I went to downtown Chicago to see for myself and discovered that we are not told the half of it. Though not a public holiday, the centre of the city was taken up for most of the morning with a parade, led by the city fathers, all stepping out proudly. Gerry Cronin the Irish Minister for Defence was the guest of honour and walked with Daley and his mayoral party. The unbroken white line down the centre of the street was painted green, white horses in the procession were dyed green, green dye had been put in the river and some of the pubs served green beer.

The crowd, people of all ethnic origins including African and Hispanic Americans, wore some green item of clothing, while some dressed entirely in green, and most had large sprigs of various kinds of vegetation in their lapels: parsley, broccoli and even cabbage leaves. It didn't seem to matter so long as it was green. Everybody is Irish for the day. Perhaps some real Irish people had shamrock sent by a relative in Ireland. When the parade was over there was a buzz in the city and the pubs did a roaring trade.

When I arrived home Hilary told me how her friends at work had given her a hard time because she wasn't wearing anything green and wasn't sporting green vegetable matter. Tom our librarian friend had invited us out for a drink that evening and we were to meet him at 'Jimmies', the famous pub on campus with minimal basic wooden tables and chairs, and a great atmosphere. Faculty, students, staff, local 'hard hats' and bums all frequented 'Jimmies'.

It was a dive with class. When we arrived Tom bought us a drink and then decided we had to go. He took us to the rooms of Brent House, the Anglican Society Centre, where he had arranged a surprise St Patrick's Day party for us. He had assembled student friends, and as soon as we arrived they presented us each with a green carnation. They had no idea of the significance of the green carnation in its association with Oscar Wilde. You can imagine my embarrassment when they called on me to dance an Irish jig. Again Hilary and I let ourselves down; we were the only ones not wearing something green, apart from the carnations.

Towards the end of our time in Chicago I met an Anglican priest at a gathering of Episcopal clergy. He was from an old New England family, and was on the Anglo-Catholic wing of the Church. He lived on his own in a large apartment in Hyde Park and invited us to dinner. When we arrived he greeted us and introduced us to two young men who were like acolytes and served the meal, which was a fine one with a liberal supply of good wine, a different one with each course. After dinner he invited Hilary, since she was the only woman present, to join the gentlemen for port. When we were thinking of going home he announced that he wanted to bring us to a pub he knew in an Irish district of the city.

Leaving the two young men behind we got into his car and after about half an hour arrived at the pub on the other side of town. It was long and narrow with a high wooden counter down one side on which there was, in a prominent position, a large collection box for the IRA. The floor was bare boards and at the far end of the bar there was a pot-bellied solid fuel stove. The pub was full, almost entirely of men, most of whom looked like construction workers. Hilary particularly felt conspicuous, and so did I as the only man wearing a collar and tie. Our host, who was wearing his clerical collar, was no doubt taken for a Roman Catholic priest. He bought us Gaelic coffees and eventually we left and he delivered us home in the best of order after a long night.

A couple of days later we phoned to thank him and arranged a date some weeks hence for him to come to us for dinner. The night arrived, the meal was prepared, but on a somewhat more modest scale than his – there was one wine, a red Californian *vin ordinaire*, our standard tipple. He was late and we waited. When he was the best part of an hour overdue we phoned. There was no reply. We waited and phoned again. Still no reply. He never turned up and we didn't hear from him or see him again. We both had the distinct impression that when he invited me to dinner in the first place he didn't know I had a wife.

I learned an immense amount during my time in Chicago. However, I was restricted in my studies to the courses that were given, most of which were highly academic, so after the year I was no further on with my questions about the Christian faith. When the time came to leave Chicago we contemplated going west and travelling home via the Far East. In the end we decided not to and arrived home in June 1971. In August I was appointed rector of the parish of Stradbally, Co Laois.

8

The Midlands

Stradbally is roughly half way between Portlaoise and Athy in prosperous farming country; not that any farmer would admit to prosperity. On the road from Portlaoise the long straight street of the village falls before you and rises again at the far end towards the Windy Gap and, in the distance, a spectacular view of the Wicklow hills. The name comes from the Irish, *sráid bhaile*, literally 'street town', meaning village. It was an apt name for Stradbally which was just that; a single wide street, at one end of which was Court Square, with a fine nineteenth century limestone courthouse, now used as a branch library and County Council offices.

It was a moderately sized village with two churches, a convent, a malting, a chemist, two garages, two butchers, two undertakers and six pubs. With exceptions, allegiance to a particular butcher or undertaker could reveal a family's politics. Similarly in most Irish villages drinking Protestants, or rather those who drink in public, tend to drink in Fine Gael pubs, and that was the case in Stradbally.

My predecessor was Walton Empey who had been appointed to Limerick as Dean, and eventually became, as he described himself later, 'the low flying' Archbishop of Dublin. Walton was a lovely human being, devout without being pious but not in the first rank of administrators. He was a kind and faithful pastor, a devotee of contemplative prayer and committed to the daily offices of the Church. The nuns in the convent told me that he even out-prayed them! Walton had said Morning Prayer in the parish church every morning; the practice of some traditional Anglican churchmen.

In all the time of my training for ministry, despite attendance at the daily offices while a student in residence during the final two years before ordination, nobody ever told me that to say Morning and Evening Prayer daily in a parish was *de rigueur*. The daily offices were not said in St John's where I had been curate. To say the office privately in one's study was one thing; it could be a valuable discipline for clergy of a certain temperament, but it wasn't something I had ever done. I performed my private devotions in my own peculiar way. I did not have a commitment to say the office in the parish church every morning, when there would be nobody else present or there might be one or two who came simply because it was on or to support the rector. Clergy who do say the office daily in church see it as a witness to the world when the bell is rung – a statement that the Church is alive and well and at prayer, and praying for the world. It is also an opportunity for parishioners to attend formal worship during the week at times of need or crisis in their lives. The daily office, however, was not part of the Church of Ireland in which I was brought up. I could not have kept up that kind of discipline because I wasn't convinced of its value, so when I arrived in Stradbally I dropped the daily office and nobody that I knew of registered an objection.

Apart from that, I was lucky, as Walton had left the parish in good heart. He had also involved himself in organisations in the village, and had helped to develop excellent ecumenical relations in the community, both of which I looked forward to building on. These were the days when the effects of the Second Vatican Council were beginning to be felt in parishes around the country; when openness and inclusiveness were the order of the day and when the small Protestant community was, in large part, responding enthusiastically to local ecumenism.

In communities in rural Ireland before the early 1960s and the Second Vatican Council, relations between the Protestant and Roman Catholic people were in the main good. There was neighbourliness between families and especially in the farming community when neighbours helped each other at critical seasons of the year. The parishes, however, kept a respectful distance; there was almost no coming and going between them. By the time I arrived in Stradbally, thanks to good Pope John XXIII, there was a new atmosphere abroad that encouraged cooperation between the traditions and encouraged the Churches to do things together. Most people of both Churches supported this, but I have no doubt there was a small number of Roman Catholics who still saw Protestants as heretics to be kept at arm's length. There was also a small number of Protestants who thought that ecumenical developments were not desirable as they would mean their small community was in danger of being swamped.

There is, even today, within Church of Ireland country parishes a range of opinion about relationships with Roman Catholics. Most want the rector to forge good relations across the traditional divide and are glad of any activities that break down barriers and build up trust. At the other end of the spectrum there are parishioners who see the rector as the man or woman whose duty it is to be the public and official face of their distinctiveness, apartness, and even for some, their superiority to the majority.

In Stradbally I saw it as important to co-operate with the Catholic clergy and parish when possible and help to break down old prejudices and respond warmly and positively to every ecumenical opportunity that presented itself. I saw it as my job to lead the Church of Ireland community in that direction and to build on the ecumenical work my predecessor had begun. For example I was invited to attend a Mass, celebrated by Bishop Lennon, at the Mass rock in the heart of Oakvale Wood outside the village where in penal times fugitive priests said Mass. I was robed and stood behind the altar with the other priests. When the bishop had taken off his robes after the Mass he came straight over to me, welcomed me and thanked me for coming.

Two of the former three Anglo-Irish estates on which the village was centred still survived, though greatly diminished in size as a result of the Land Acts. One family had been titled but lost the title after one generation in the eighteenth century when the title-holder died without issue. They had an enormous Victorian house, the original having been destroyed by fire, and only a small amount of arable land, on which it was difficult to survive, but survive they did. They were very British and on significant occasions would toast the Queen. The old major was a gentleman. He was somewhat fey and what the Irish countryman might describe as 'a relict of auld dacency'. He was exempt from joining the queue for his Sunday papers sold from the back of a car on the Main Street; the paper man handed him out his papers from the front seat while the hoi polloi queued at the back.

His son, who was in charge at the Hall, seemed to be more interested in alternative methods of doing ordinary things than in farming, much of which he left to his hard-working wife. He liked to do things like demonstrating how to heat radiators from heaps of manure and during the oil crises in the 1970s fuelling his central heating system with bales of straw or rubber tyres. The family in some ways still lived in the nineteenth century but they were accepted in the village for what they were. The village, however, lived firmly in the twentieth century. Compared with former days the family was in decline and the village was in the ascendant.

The family of the other estate, which was slightly outside the village, was a different kettle of fish. They had a somewhat more manageable house and a fine acreage of arable land that they worked industriously as a modern farm. They lived in the present and were a good example of the maxim 'to adapt is to survive.' The current adult generation of both these families had gone to school in England, the boys to Eton, while the children of the first family also went to England and the children of the second went to school in Ireland.

In the village most people were able to make a living, from Nora the local doctor, whose parents had both been doctors before her and who had a brother and sister doctors, to Seán who worked locally for the County Council. A community is made up of all sorts and conditions of people who, at the end of the day, though independent, rely on each other in all kinds of ways that they often don't realise.

The local doctor gets to know people every bit as well if not, in some circumstances, better than the clergy. These were the early days of Nora's return to Stradbally to take over the family practice and she hadn't yet trained her patients into her way of working. Farmers from out the country would come into the village on Saturday night and when the pub closed one of them might wander up to the doctor's house around midnight with some minor complaint and get Nora out of bed. Whether it was sheer inconsiderateness or they needed the night's drinking to give them courage to consult the doctor, especially a young woman doctor, I do not know.

Nora was not yet back in the village when Hilary or I first needed a doctor and we asked a parishioner to suggest one. He recommended a doctor in Portarlington, fourteen miles away; a Protestant! When Nora came home to the practice we transferred to her, primarily because we knew she was a good doctor and secondly she was in the village. It soon transpired that she looked after the whole family without charge, and couldn't be persuaded to take a fee: 'My parents never charged the Convent, the Parochial House or the Rectory,' she said, 'and I'm not going to start'.

Nora's mother, in her day, examined patients wearing white cotton gloves. There was one cottage outside the village with three bachelor brothers that Nora soon discovered she simply could not visit. She was allergic to flea bites and she came up in weals after a call there. She delegated her assistant to look after the medical care of those three gentlemen. In another cottage up the hill there was a man who when he married moved in to live with his wife, her mother and her sister. Nora was never sure which of the women he was talking about because he never referred to any of them by name. She finally tumbled to it when she realised that he was actually consistent in his references to them; he referred to them as, 'herself', his wife, 'the auld one', her mother, and 'the other one', her sister.

People who do essential and critical jobs in a community are sometimes taken for granted. If you need a doctor or a solicitor you may be able to wait a week or two for an appointment, but if the water supply fails or the sewage backs up you may need help immediately. Seán was the County Council man on the ground. He was in charge of the water and the sewage and when not involved with these essential services, he supervised a man with a horse and cart, who kept the village free of litter and the detritus of public houses and sweet shops.

In the morning on my way back from the shop with my paper I might meet Seán leaning on his shovel and stop for a chat. One morning I was saying something to him, when in the middle of a sentence he turned and walked away, and rooted with his shovel at the grass in the cracks on the footpath. I thought something I said had mortally offended him until I saw Joe O'Grady's Citroen passing on his way to his office in the Court House. Joe, Seán's boss, was the County Engineer for the area and Seán's antennae had picked him up when his car appeared at the top of the town.

It is hard to escape the conclusion that in a small community the customs of a new family at the rectory are commented on, or at least noticed. Hilary and I would not be prepared to allow local practice to determine where we shopped but we would go where we got the best value and the best service. Hilary settled down as a customer of John Donohue, the new young Fianna Fáil butcher rather than the butcher who had been Protestant in the previous generation. I bought my petrol and had my car serviced at Farrelly's garage rather than the Protestant garage, where the service was not as companionable and which was due to move to Portlaoise imminently anyway.

Ben, Teddy and Paddy Farrelly ran the garage at the top of the town. Ben did the servicing and repairs, Teddy mended punctures and fitted tyres and Paddy looked after the pumps. Paddy was particularly affable and he enjoyed conversation and the exchange of news while he served petrol and when he had finished at the pumps before he returned to the 'office', he would look up and down the street to keep an eye on the goings-on of the village.

Paddy pitched his conversation perfectly to each of his local customers and was unfailingly polite, at least to me. Above all he often had a humorous comment to make; it wasn't what he said, it was the way he put it. Country people from tillage areas are aware of the importance of dry weather after a wet spell at harvest-time.

During one such dry, sunny day after rain, when every combine harvester in the countryside was working overtime, I pulled in to the pumps for petrol and made some predictable comment about the great weather for the harvest: 'You wouldn't want to fall down in a corn-field today,' Paddy came back, 'or you'd end up in the maltings.'

I enjoyed these interludes while I was getting petrol and somehow the habit became established between us that I would purposely drop into the conversation an unusual or long word. Paddy's response was always to cup his hand behind his ear and say: 'What's that sir?' I would explain and he would say: 'Thank you sir.' It was a game of light relief we played.

The Church of Ireland church and the Roman Catholic church stood on the Main Street on either side of the entrance to Church Lane, half way up which was the rectory. Beyond the rectory there were two council estates, and when the first of these had been built Church Lane became Church Avenue. Bill and Sheila Deegan and family lived immediately opposite the rectory. Bill was a tall well-built man in his mid-thirties who farmed land close to the village and rented the parish glebe land. He was slow moving; plenty of time to stop and talk and he had the quickest wit of anybody I have known.

One day I pulled in to Farrelly's garage for petrol. Paddy was talking to Bill at the top of the forecourt and Ben served me. Ben was quiet and kindly, but I didn't have the same rapport with him that I had with Paddy. When I had paid for the petrol I went over and spoke to Paddy and Bill and as was my custom I dropped in the big word. Paddy came back with his usual: 'What's that sir?' At which Bill looked down imperiously at him and declaimed: 'God, Farrelly you're terrible ignorant, we talk like that all the time up our way.'

Not all our conversations were lightweight; occasionally a religious, as distinct from a denominational, topic might arise for mention between us. One day out of the blue, without any preliminaries, Paddy put the question to me: 'Do you believe there's anything after death?'

'I have great difficulty believing it,' I replied, trying to be honest, but not being entirely so.

'Well, I don't believe there is,' Paddy said.

'Why is that?' I enquired.

'Before your time in Stradbally there was a fellow I used to drink with every Friday night and we often talked about that kind of thing. One night we made a pact that whichever of us died first, if there was life after death, would come back to let the other know. He died a couple of years ago and he never showed.'

Before we left Stradbally an uncle died and left Paddy a fine farm in Co Meath. Though claiming little or no knowledge of farming he could not pass up the opportunity and made the career change, not that he thought in terms of careers. Despite having married and having a young son, Paddy was lonely on the farm in Meath and missed the pumps. The night-time company in his local pub was not as congenial as it had been in Stradbally, so for the first couple of years he came back on any excuse and would spend a few hours at the pumps and catch up with the latest news, gossip and scandal of the village.

The parish priest for all of my time in Stradbally was Fr Mahon, an elderly gentleman, whose great passion was coursing greyhounds. He put me to shame when I, in my car, the best part of forty years his junior, would meet him walking his dogs miles out of the village, further than I would ever walk. He was always friendly when we met and cooperative in matters that affected both of us. He called me 'your reverence', which I took as his way of being respectful to what I stood for. Catholic people have this problem of not wanting to call Protestant clergy 'Mr' since to them it seems disrespectful, so they most commonly use 'reverend'. I would have preferred if he had called me by my Christian name; what could be more appropriate? He was, however, of the old school and such informality and the relaxations of the Second Vatican Council had come too late for him to change.

One day talking together about the stresses of the work we both did, he ended by telling me how lucky I was to have a wife to go home to. When it came to a proposal to set up a group of Roman

Catholic and Church of Ireland parishioners to discuss ecumenical issues Fr Mahon did not take part himself but he was perfectly happy for his curate, Fr Ned Aughney, to do so.

The Presentation sisters gave Hilary and me a particularly warm welcome when we arrived in Stradbally. They were still coming to terms with their new freedoms that resulted from the Second Vatican Council. In the convent there were elderly sisters who had lived most of their lives under the old rules and found the adjustment difficult and there were younger sisters who adapted readily. I am always surprised when I discover lay people who think that all clergy are the same in what they believe and think, and yet up to this time I used to make the same mistake myself about nuns. I soon discovered that amongst the sisters there were conservative ones with closed attitudes and progressive ones ready to be open. In the ecumenical groups we had some of each.

One night we were discussing our respective positions on the eucharist, teasing out differences and discovering common ground. Every time we came to some agreement one of the nuns would say: 'Yes, but ye haven't got the Mass'. One of the other nuns would point out to her that that was exactly what we were discussing and the discussion would continue. As soon as there was some agreement on another point she would want to bring it to a close again with: 'Yes, but ye haven't got the Mass'. We'd all try again to help her to see the issues and at the first sniff of finding some common ground, out she would come again with: 'Yes, but ye haven't got the Mass', to the utter frustration of her colleagues from the convent.

Another night in the group the delicate subject of sex arose. There was general agreement that sex outside marriage was not a good idea but this was not enough for one of the sisters. She recounted, albeit in veiled language but her meaning was clear, that her sister-in-law, now that she had completed her family, had decided to give up sex altogether, and ended her story with: 'Isn't that lovely?' The Prods in the group were struck dumb, but one of the other nuns, better versed in the ways of the world than her sister in religion, was embarrassed: 'You might think it's lovely,' she said, 'but I doubt if your brother does.'

I marvelled that this Augustinian view of marital sex should be alive and well in rural Ireland towards the end of the twentieth century.

The position of superior in the convent rotated every three years. When one of the more progressive sisters was superior she tried to implement the spirit of the Vatican Council and exercise a democratic way of working. Rather than hand down decisions she tried to achieve consensus. One day she asked one of the sisters for her view on some matter or other to be told with impatience to get on and make the decision herself and give up her Protestant ways!

Mother Patrick from Wexford Town where I had been born and brought up, and Mother Finbar, as you might guess, from Cork, where my mother was from, were two of the oldest members of the convent. I had much in common with them both and we got on particularly well. When Mother Finbar died I went down to the convent to offer my condolences. I was welcomed in and brought up to the room where she was laid out. The curtains were drawn and the only light in the room was from candles. There were two sisters sitting on chairs keeping vigil and telling their beads. Now Protestants are often found wanting when confronted with a corpse, so I went over to the bed, looked at Mother Finbar, bowed my head and said a prayer, probably for her community who would miss her, as I could never get my head theologically around praying for the dead. When I finished I went back and sat down beside the sister who had accompanied me upstairs. I tried to find something appropriate to say to avoid the trite, 'Doesn't she look well,' and failed. I was prepared to endure a silence rather than say something gauche so there was a long silence that the sister beside me ended: 'Did you ever see a dead nun before?' she asked impishly. I had to admit that I hadn't.

The convent employed a man to milk the cow they kept for the house. Billy was an affable rogue who told a story well and with a great turn of phrase. He was a most congenial man who smiled easily and his inevitable response to something surprising or unusual or even to some new piece of information was, 'Be the scatterin' eucalyptus!' Mother Anthony was fond of Billy and used to leave a nip of whiskey under an upturned bowl on the table in the kitchen for him when he finished the evening milking. When to arrive home from the pub after a few too many was going to be bad news, Billy would go around the back of the convent, climb up on top of the hay in the shed and sleep it off.

Billy used to do some odd jobs for me around the rectory grounds and before he started work it was absolutely necessary to spend the first ten minutes or so listening to his stories in order to get the best from him. This was no employer/employee relationship; it was more like a contest of wits. Like many men of a similar kind Billy needed to affirm that his distinctive expertise was a skill in which his employer was entirely deficient. One of the jobs he did for me was to dig a trench from the yard under a wall into the garden to lay on a water supply. When he arrived with his shovel his eye fell on a shovel I had bought some time before in the local hardware shop to do some small job. It was a good implement, lighter than his with a varnished and tapered handle. Billy picked it up, felt the weight, examined the shovel and put it down: 'That's a shovel for a woman', he pronounced. I left him to the work and later that afternoon when I went out to see him he was using the woman's shovel and he continued to use it for the rest of the job.

When it came to paying him Billy and I indulged in a game. His terms of employment were never specified but I paid him the going agricultural labourer's rate. At the end of the week or the end of the job I'd ask him how many hours he had worked. Billy would stand erect, lean on the shovel and after counting up in his head he'd give me a figure that was always a few hours more than I knew he had worked. I would go into the house and come out with the money and say: 'That's so many hours', quoting the figure he had given me and hand him the money that I had computed at the agricultural rate for the time he actually did work. He never queried this; to do so would have been beneath his dignity.

Billy and Molly, his wife, lived in one of the council estates beyond the rectory. Billy drove an ancient Farina Austin 1300 that bounced up and down Church Avenue for want of new shock absorbers. He informed his drinking companions that he kept a clean windscreen, that is, he didn't pay car tax. He drank in a 'Protestant' pub in the village and used to regale my parishioners and all and sundry with my idiosyncrasies. I was greatly amused when I heard them back and was impressed by his powers of observation. Just before I left Stradbally Billy was taken to Portlaoise Hospital with a clot in his leg. I went to see him and he told me in no uncertain terms that the doctors didn't know what they were talking about. In fact it transpired he was right. He had a torn muscle. I never heard, but I can imagine the entertainment in the pub on his first night back.

Portlaoise was the local county hospital where most patients from Stradbally went. The matron was Sister de Lellis, a nun who combined a strong spiritual sense with a down-to-earth understanding of human nature and an acute sense of humour. She smiled and laughed easily but nonetheless did the business. From time to time she would 'phone me to ask me to pray for some intractable problem she was coping with, without ever letting me know what the problem was. Her attitude was, 'The Lord will know what you're talking about.' I had an instinct that most of these problems were not to do with patients but with the fraught relationship between some of the senior medical staff. If I were in the hospital shortly after one of these calls she had a coded way of letting me know if the Lord had intervened or if he was still considering the matter.

My mother lived with us for the second half of our time in Stradbally and was in indifferent health. She had numerous hospital stays in Portlaoise and in the Mater in Dublin. In her eighties she felt, as she said herself, that she was a damn nuisance to us and believed strongly it was time she was gone. 'There's really nothing more for me to do and if it weren't for the disgrace it would be to you I'd put my head in the oven.' She wasn't depressed and said this in a matter of fact way. Before an operation in the Mater, and knowing her heart wasn't good she convinced herself that she would die under the anaesthetic and this pleased her greatly as it would be a clean and easy way to go. In fact she survived and woke with nurses at her bed calling her name to bring her round. She looked up and realising she was back in the ward, she floored them with: 'Oh no, I don't believe it, I'm not still here?' It was because of the religious nursing sisters at the Mater and Sister de Lellis in Portlaoise that my mother, instructed me in her old age: 'If I need hospital and I'm too sick to decide, send me where there are nuns.'

When we arrived in Stradbally in August 1971 things in the north of Ireland were bad. In March James Chichester-Clark had resigned and Brian Faulkner succeeded him as Prime Minister. During the summer Provisional IRA violence had increased. There was a cycle of bombings, shootings and rioting all over the north, particularly in West Belfast. On 9 August Faulkner introduced internment that led to the worst violence in Republican areas since August 1969. This led to some Loyalist paramilitary retaliation, and by the end of 1971 there was no sign of any abatement of the violence.

Then on Sunday 30 January 1972 British troops shot dead thirteen men, members of a civil rights march in Derry – Bloody Sunday. The whole country was shocked, and next day there were violent protests all over Northern Ireland. In the south a national day of mourning was declared and on 2 February a huge demonstration of people marched on the British Embassy in Dublin and set it on fire.

I have a vivid memory of walking down to the village on Monday morning, the day after Bloody Sunday, to get my paper and wondering how local Catholics viewed me and their Protestant neighbours. I knew that thoughtful and educated Catholics did not make the identification that Protestant equals British but I was equally aware that some prejudiced and uneducated Catholics did. These were tense times when Protestants around the south of Ireland, particularly in country areas, felt distinctly uncomfortable, despite the fact that only a minuscule number of them would have felt in any sense British. The great majority were as outraged at the killings in Derry as their Catholic neighbours were. Some parishioners spoke to me around this time of feeling some strain with Catholic neighbours whose families had lived beside each other for generations. It was hard to know how much of this was real or how much imagined. No incidents occurred and in due course these sensitivities disappeared. Some years later in our ecumenical groups we discussed this kind of issue when the point was made and understood that Protestant did not equal either Paisley or British.

In small communities in rural Ireland clergy of all denominations, by reason of their office, have traditionally been afforded some deference. Sometimes this has been obsequious and unhealthy. In moderation it can be useful when clergy of one denomination or another are elected to chair organisations or committees in the community. With a clerical chairman there is usually a built-in neutrality and capacity to avoid contention and promote consensus. In Stradbally I was elected chairman of the Tidy Towns Committee, on which were some worthy citizens. During the years I was chairman we didn't win anything in the competition but we did bring some improvements to the village, especially the planting of trees. It amazed me that so many people are unaware of environmental issues, especially matters like litter and the value of a lick of paint. I believe that the committee began to raise awareness on these issues but like any other matter of community importance there were some who were enthusiastic and others who couldn't care less.

One night I was sitting in my study when there was a ring at the rectory door. It was Ger who owned one of the local pubs. His brother was a professor of obstetrics and he had a nephew who was a nationally known journalist. Ger had inherited the family pub and stayed in Stradbally. He also drove the hearse for his sister-in-law, one of the undertakers in the village. Neither of these jobs stretched Ger's talents. He was an avid reader of Zane Gray western novels and once picked up an inconsistency and wrote to the author to point it out. In his reply the author said that Ger was the first person ever to pick up a flaw in his books that revealed he had never lived in cowboy country and in fact was a city dweller. Ger was proud of this.

Ger planned to revive the boxing club for the boys of the village and the purpose of his visit was to ask me to be president. J.B. Evans Gregory, one of my predecessors as rector, had been president of the boxing club at the time of its demise many years before, and he thought it would be good if I lent my name to the revival of the club. He assured me that there was no committee work or fund raising involved. All I had to do was lend my moral support. I agreed and a week or two later I put in an appearance at the hall one night when some of the youngsters were training. The boxing club never properly got off the ground and that was the last I heard of it.

It is easy, if you have the will, to become involved in the life of a small community; not only to take part in its celebrations but to be affected by its tragedies. If somebody is killed in an accident a pall hangs over the village for days and even longer. Community mourning is a support for the bereaved family at the time, but eventually people move on, life returns to normal and the bereaved family is left to grieve on their own.

There was a Catholic man who, when I met him around the village, always stopped to talk. He was a farmer, but a man with an interest in most things and with educated opinions on many. He was good company. When he died I called to see his widow, who I didn't know, a few days after his funeral. She welcomed me in and before I said a word, as we sat down she told me politely but firmly that while Mick had faith, she did not believe in religion and she certainly didn't believe in life after death. We had a fascinating discussion during which she discovered that we had more in common than she thought.

Apart from the funerals of Church of Ireland parishioners, Hilary and I would attend the funerals of neighbours from the houses further up Church Avenue at the Catholic Church. At the funeral of a woman we knew well, who had lived a few doors away from the rectory, the curate Dinny Doran saw me in the church as the procession with the coffin came down the aisle. He stopped the procession and called me out of the congregation to process with him and the parish priest. On another occasion I was invited to read a lesson at the funeral Mass of a man with whose family we had become friends. These were important developments in community relations in rural Ireland in the 1970s that would not have happened ten years before.

One local man, however, who had spent some years in Australia, told me that in Ireland we took death and funerals much too seriously. One morning in Australia he and his friend arrived down to breakfast in their digs to discover that the man of the house had died during the night. They went back upstairs immediately and put on collars and ties and their good suits. A few minutes later the son of the house arrived down in his working clothes and when he had finished his breakfast, he collected his lunch box and went off to work. My friend strengthened his contention by recounting that in his local town in Australia a bank customer dropped dead while making a lodgement. The teller and the next customer in the queue began to argue about whether the lodgement had been completed or not before he died while others called the ambulance and looked after the body on the floor.

Around this time there was the beginnings of the demystification of the clergy of all traditions. Lay Catholics in particular were becoming less deferential and more ready to think for themselves. In a small country church of a neighbouring parish, at the time of the annual dues, the parish priest used to stand at the centre of the front of the church holding a large alms dish. The congregation filed up one aisle, placed their contribution on the dish and went down the other aisle. On the first such Sunday after Michael's mother died Michael lined up, put his contribution on the dish and was on his way down when the priest called him: 'Oh, Michael.'

'Yes, Father.'

'Your mother, God be good to her, used to give £x at this collection.'

Michael looked the priest straight in the eye and said: 'Well Father, she'll give it no more', and continued on his way. No undue deference there.

Church of Ireland parishioners, by and large, worked hard for their parish, and many of them played their full part in the broader community. Some were private kinds of people and no matter what religion they were they wouldn't have been involved in village life. There were of course private kinds of Roman Catholics too who didn't become involved in the life of the village.

As my own theological views developed I tried to encourage parishioners to think, to see their religious practice not just as habit, blind obedience to tradition or as an affirmation of their distinctiveness from the majority religious community. Rather to see it as something to explore in order to better use it as a support in their daily lives and an insight into their value system. With most parishioners this was something of an uphill struggle; most of them did not think theologically. Now to 'think theologically' sounds horribly pretentious but in fact it simply describes what we do when we think about God at all. Where is he? How can you know God? Does he intervene in the world, and if so how? Who was Jesus Christ? How can he have been both God and man? And many other questions of a similar kind. These kinds of questions fascinated me and in my innocence I thought they would interest parishioners.

In a way that town people can never understand, the weather is of vital importance to farmers. If it is raining when they want fine weather or dry when they want rain, you'll hear all about it. When the weather is perfect you never hear a word, but since farmers' needs change so often that situation never lasts for long. This is a prelude to telling you that from time to time at critical seasons of the year, mostly sowing in spring and harvesting in the autumn, farmers would ask me to pray for rain or for fine weather.

I used to ask them did they really believe in a God up above the bright blue sky that would intervene in the weather if we prayed hard or often enough. The often indignant answer to this was almost invariably 'Yes'. One parishioner told me that he was cutting corn one harvest and as he was finishing his last field dark rain clouds gathered. He prayed to God to hold off the rain until he finished, and God did. It stayed fine until he had cut the last bit, and then he saw the first drops of rain on the windscreen of the cab before the heavens opened. Another man told me he believed that God intervened in the weather, and looking downwards he put his hands back-to-back and motioned outwards with them showing how God would push back the clouds. I didn't ask him to demonstrate what kind of motion God would use to draw the clouds together when someone asked him for rain.

It was hard to blame the person in the pew for holding these views since there were prayers in the Church of Ireland Book of Common Prayer for rain and for fine weather. The prayer for rain asks only for 'moderate rain and showers', I suppose on the principle that too much of a good thing is bad, while the other prayer asks, not for fine weather, but for 'fair weather'; classic examples of the moderation of Anglicanism! I used to tell parishioners that I didn't believe in a God that intervened in the weather to fill the coffers of well-heeled farmers in Co Laois, when he did nothing for thousands of people in Africa who were dying of starvation as a result of drought. Nobody ever took me up on this.

I tried to get them to think about this kind of issue and to talk about their image of God. I never got very far but word came back to me that people found my attitude somewhat disturbing and I became known to some people as 'the rector who wouldn't pray for rain'. One Sunday I preached a sermon on the weather in which I presented the issues gently. I tried to show that since the seventeenth century when the Book of Common Prayer was compiled our understanding of the world had changed because of science and our image of God must change too. I asked them to think about it and talk to me about it when we met. After the service, a woman came over to me outside the church. She was smiling and, not the slightest bit upset by the sermon, she said: 'We don't care what you think, we're going to go on praying for the weather, because when we do, we feel better.' She had made an important theological point that I agree with. In my view that, rather than intervention, is what intercessory prayer is about.

The extent to which I believed that the average parishioner needed some adult education was illustrated for me one day when I brought communion to a housebound parishioner. A bachelor, he lived on his own and wasn't well; I had been bringing communion to him every month for some time. This day I arrived as usual and while I was chatting to him and laying out the vessels I happened to glance up and see on the wall the most garish Italianate picture of the Sacred Heart. When we had finished the communion I glanced up at the picture and said casually: 'Jack, I see you have a new picture.'

'I have,' he said. 'I must tell you about that.'

I waited, curious to hear the explanation.

'A fella' came to the door selling holy pictures, and when I saw them I asked him had he no Protestant ones, and he said he had and went back to the van and brought me that.'

Jack must have done a lot of his shopping from travelling salesmen. He suffered terribly with his stomach, but he had no teeth. Tentatively one day I suggested to him that if he could chew he might be able to eat food that would help his stomach and maybe false teeth would help.

'Go way owa that,' he said, 'I bought a set of them from a fella' at the door and they went up in heap in me head.'

It must be said, however, that if you were in trouble with a heifer calving you couldn't have the help of a better man than Jack.

All these people made up the colourful tapestry that was life in Stradbally. And of course there were many more. There was Jimmy who had sat at the back of the class at school with Seán, the County Council's man on the ground, and stuck pellets of chewed paper onto the ceiling, left school early, and now owned one of the finest stone works in Ireland. I once asked him if he regretted not working at school: 'Not at all, if I had worked I might have ended up an assistant county engineer in somewhere like Leitrim or Longford.'

There was the charming Merc-driving Humphrey, making a mint from, amongst other things, his graveyard of lorry wrecks. Isaac, who could do anything with his hands and came back from England, built a shed that became a factory and supplied ladders to the P&T and the ESB, and still called it 'the shed'. Babs, the best teller of a story I ever met; hardware merchant, newsagent and undertaker. Michael the grocer with Mollie his wife and a pub in Waterford. Joe the blacksmith's son who built trailers for farmers, and Ken who repaired machinery and shot clay pigeons for Ireland. Jim the County Councillor with the game ankle, and Mick his nephew who ran the Post Office. Christy, the guard, who'd summon his grandmother. Paddy Gaff and 'The Blood' Lawlor in the autumn of their lives, who in their day were brought to court and fined for poaching rabbits in the Hall. There was also, inevitably, the darker side of life in the village, largely hidden, unspoken and unseen.

There comes a time for clergy when they have done all they can do in a parish, given their own particular aptitudes and gifts and it is good for them to move on. Some do and some don't. After eleven years I felt I had nothing new to give so in the summer of 1982 I left Stradbally and was appointed Church of Ireland Adult Education Officer, based at the former Hostel, now the Theological College in Rathgar. Hilary and I had spent eleven happy years in Stradbally and during that time our two children Sarah and Ben had arrived. They attended the local Church of Ireland school where Miss Taylor had taught generations of Protestant children in one small room. It was an excellent start to their education. We were all sad to leave Stradbally but I looked forward to a stimulating time at the college. I hoped that a different kind of challenge would give me a new edge and maybe somebody would put me right on some of my theological difficulties.

9

Adult Education

The Church of Ireland Theological College in Rathgar evolved from the Divinity Hostel that originally provided residential accommodation in Dublin for Church of Ireland ordinands. By the time I arrived there in 1982 it had become a full-scale college for the training of clergy for the Church of Ireland in conjunction with Trinity.

Training for Church of Ireland ordinands is divided into three parts: academic, pastoral and devotional. The academic component includes biblical studies; Old and New Testaments, Church History, Doctrine, Liturgy, Ethics and Philosophy of Religion. The pastoral component includes study of society and all the vicissitudes of being human and the practical support of people coping with these. The devotional bit is about how to say your prayers.

Despite what some people might think, if they thought about it at all, the Bible didn't fall out of the sky one day as a message from God. The word 'Bible' comes from the Greek word *biblia* meaning books, which describes exactly what the Bible is; not a book but a collection of books, written at different times and in different places in a variety of circumstances. These are in two categories: the Old Testament books originally written largely in Hebrew and the New Testament books written originally in Greek. There are thirty-nine books in the Old Testament, written during a period of over a thousand years, and there are twenty-seven books in the New Testament written largely during the second half of the first century AD.

The Old Testament contains books of Jewish law, history, prophecy, poetry, including a beautiful erotic love poem, teachings and an apocalyptic writing. All of these books together are the literary expression of the religious life of ancient Israel.

The New Testament contains four different kinds of book: gospels, history of a particular kind (Acts), letters and an apocalyptic book. These books recount the teachings and events in the life of Jesus and who the writers believed that he was.

The unifying thread that runs through all the books of the Bible is the account of what the Church teaches us is God's self-revelation, seen through a diversity of human situations and personalities of the Hebrew tribe in the Old Testament and supremely in Jesus Christ in the New Testament. This, I believe, was a rather hit and miss way for the creator of this magnificent and mysterious universe to reveal himself to the inhabitants of this small planet, but more of this later. As a result of what the Church teaches, the Bible has an important place in the life of the Church as a source for its teaching and as an authority for its doctrine.

Study of the Bible, sometimes known as biblical criticism, is central to preparation for ordination. It looks at questions such as: 'Who wrote the books?' and 'Where, when and why were they written?' This is in order to understand what they say and what they were intended to mean in the first place, the better to apply their meaning to the present day. Some people, however, believe that the Bible is literally inspired as God's word and we should simply accept what it says at face value and not subject it to analysis of this kind.

The two periods of history that Anglican ordinands study particularly are those of the early Church and the Reformation. During the first five centuries of the Christian era General Councils of the Church laid down the main doctrines of the Church, such as the doctrine of the Trinity, usually in order to counter heresy. Some of the great Christian theological minds lived during this period, Tertullian, Origen, Augustine, not that you'd want to mind everything they said. For example Tertullian informed women: 'You are the devil's gateway', and Augustine said that women were not made in the image of God. The early Councils of the Church laid down essential doctrines, which are still the basis of orthodox, with a small 'o', Christian belief. The Reformation period is important as the time when Anglicanism defined for itself what was essential for Christian belief and what was not. The doctrine of Anglicanism is in essence the doctrine of the early Church as set out in the creeds and the early Councils of the Church. The study of doctrine itself lays particular emphasis on this period and how the Church defined who Jesus was.

The study of liturgy is the study of the evolution of worship in the life of the Church and the doctrines that lie behind it. Ethics are concerned with how to make the right decisions in the way we behave. The Bible is the ultimate authority in such matters, but the Bible, for obvious reasons, doesn't have anything directly to say on such issues as nuclear weapons, embryology and genetic engineering. Nor does it have anything directly to say on such ever-present issues as contraception and abortion. How do we know how to make right decisions in such matters? Finally amongst the subjects for academic study is philosophy of religion. This is the study of religion as a human phenomenon; the study of religion as part of human behaviour without preconceived ideas.

The second part of training for ordination is pastoral. The purpose of this is to learn how best to work with people wherever they are in their life or at whatever crisis they may be facing. Some experience is required in and some understanding of such things as education, youth work, care of the old, psychological problems, hospital and even prison work. My adult education work with ordinands came within this part of training and included both theory and practical experience by placements in parishes.

I saw it as my job to encourage students to expand their view of the Christian faith for themselves and to learn ways to help parishioners to a better understanding of how to apply faith to their daily lives. This involved looking at the principles of how adults, as opposed to children, learn, and hopefully grow and develop. The problem is that the religious educational age of most adults in the pew is somewhere around ten or twelve years of age. Their understanding of the Christian faith is the same in adulthood as it was when they were taught the basics as children. Adults may be highly educated in the professions, doctors, lawyers, scientists and others, but remain as children in their understanding of Christianity. Some may be successful in business and travel the world, but their faith is not childlike, but childish. It was my job to help future clergy to understand this and to develop ways of helping adults to grow and develop in their faith and to learn more about the Church and its teachings, the better to relate Church teaching and faith to their life in the world. With most students it was like pushing a boulder uphill. For many, being a member of the Church was simply a matter of believing and attending Church regularly – bums on comfortable pews. Unfortunately this attitude was widespread with clergy in parishes too.

Finally the third part of training is in the devotional life. That is to make each student aware of the spiritual dimension of life and to help him or her to develop their own sense of the spiritual, whatever that may be for them. I have already mentioned that in my time as a student there were some lectures on the subject and we looked at the examples of notable Anglican divines such as Jeremy Taylor. We also had what were called 'quiet days'; days of silence with a routine of chapel services and devotional talks. I found these days of silence both artificial and oppressive. Despite trying to read some kind of devotional literature that was somebody else's experience, I wanted the quiet day to end, not that I had an urge to talk, I hadn't, but I longed for the return to normality. The assumption was that everybody should benefit from quiet days, but I never felt they did me any good. How some people cope with silent retreats of a week or more I cannot fathom. I wonder if such retreats are designed to encourage the participant to sublimate their own humanity to a conventional spirituality that encourages compliant conformity.

In three years which is the normal time for ordination training, there is never enough time to do all of these things well, so Divinity students spend their time trying to cover them as best they can and doing some well and some not so well. If there were ten years for all these subjects it would still not be possible to exhaust them.

In the Church of England and in other branches of the Anglican community there are theological colleges that represent the different emphases within Anglicanism. There are low church evangelical, broad church and high church colleges. An ordinand can therefore attend a college that most closely suits his/her own churchmanship. The Church of Ireland, as a relatively small Church, has only one theological college, which therefore contains ordinands from a range of churchmanship. Although the range is not as great in the Church of Ireland as it is in other Anglican Churches. This diversity within one college leads to much debate and discussion between students and sometimes to contention that is not helped by the hothouse and in some ways unnatural religious atmosphere that such an institution creates.

Among the students in the Church of Ireland Theological College there was a range of ages, from ordinands straight from a primary degree at university, to older men with experience of the world of business, the trades or of one of the professions. Some of the younger ordinands were the sons and daughters of clergy, following in father's footsteps. It is interesting to note that recently seven out of the twelve bishops of the Church of Ireland were sons of clergy. Many of the older men were married and of necessity separated from their wives and children during the week: a less than ideal situation. Mostly they went home at weekends and fulfilled their practical requirements in their home parishes. Wives and families occasionally came to stay at the college for weekends.

The college was a cross between an academic institution and a religious community, but in reality it was neither. It was a bit of both. These cross-sections of difference were good, in that they forced people to live with diversity and to accommodate people of different theological positions from their own. Some of the students stretched the bounds of Anglicanism to the limit and in my opinion beyond. One day in banter with two extremely evangelical students, who constantly disagreed with me in lectures, and who I have no doubt didn't consider me a proper Christian, I said: 'You fellows aren't Anglicans at all, why don't you go off and start a gospel hall of your own?' They didn't challenge my contention but one of them with a smile held out his hand and rubbing his thumb and first finger together said: 'The monthly cheque.' Had the principal known that I said this to two of his men he would have been furious – all his geese were swans. He would have been quite happy that they would develop theologically by the time they came to be ordained. Many others and I knew damn well they wouldn't.

Since as Adult Education Officer part of my brief was to work outside the college promoting adult education in the parishes it meant I did not have to spend all of my time in and around the college. I travelled to parishes and to groups of clergy around the Church both north and south promoting the idea of the growth and development of adults through learning and providing practical ways of implementing them. Most clergy claimed that they hadn't time to get into all of this, much as they might have accepted it as a good thing in principle; they were too busy with the practicalities of administering their parishes. Some, however, did and, I believe, found it a valuable development in their parishes, albeit with a small minority of parishioners.

When I arrived at the college the principal asked me to become manager of the small training studio that had fallen into disuse and to revive it for use with students and clergy for teaching communication skills. I knew nothing about television and video and went on a course to a media-training centre in England where I learned the basics and developed the use of the studio with the help of some interested students who were competent in electronics.

Apart from courses for students we ran in-service training for clergy at the studio. Over the years I have discovered that some experienced professional media people, at home with microphone or camera, are extremely nervous and ill at ease facing a live audience. I discovered the opposite to be true for some clergy who, used to a live audience, are badly thrown by a camera. One older rector in the studio, though assured that he wasn't going out live on national television but only onto a tape, shook before the camera and stuttered and stammered his way through his presentation. I would not have been surprised to find a pool on the floor when he had gone. Another was even more nervous. When I approached him after he ended his piece he kept saying: 'Sorry, thank you, sorry, sorry, thank you' as he backed away tripping over a chair and out the studio door. These were both experienced senior clergy who stood up and addressed a live congregation every Sunday.

While I was at the college, and for some years after, Hilary was the college domestic administrator. As any clergyman or minister of religion will testify the salary of a working wife, a perk not available to a Catholic priest, is a welcome supplement to the clerical stipend to augment the family finances. We lived not far from the college in Templeogue and Sarah and Ben went to the local large Church of Ireland National School in Rathfarnham, a big change from the one teacher school in Stradbally. From there they went on to Wesley College.

Hilary was responsible for running the catering and accommodation end of the house. During her time there were two principals, both of whom were Professors of Pastoral Theology, neither of whom was an experienced parochial clergyman. For some of the students, especially the engaged and married ones, Hilary became a listening ear and an unofficial pastoral counsellor. On more than one occasion she brought students home with her for the night to talk and to have a break from the college.

For my work with clergy and parishes around the country I was responsible to The Adult Education Council of the Church which brought me in contact with the administrative centre of the Church of Ireland at Church House, Rathmines. Both Church House and the Church of Ireland College of Education, where primary school teachers were trained, moved out to Rathmines in the 1960s from Stephen's Green and Kildare Street respectively.

In Church House an efficient civil service administered the Church at large. It was a fine body of highly respectable men and women, in those days all Church of Ireland by denomination, if not by conviction. There was a touch of 'the old school tie' about recruitment. The King's Hospital was particularly well represented on the staff. On the face of it, it was all very gentlemanly, however, I recommended to a staff member, who had been in my year in school, that he ought to join a trade union. I told him that if push came to shove, and times were tough, staff might have to be laid off and he ought to have somebody to fight his corner. He thought I was joking and informed me solemnly that there was a staff association. He never did join a union. He survived and has since retired.

Periodically during the year Church of Ireland clergy and laity from the four corners of Ireland converge on Church House. Over two or three days of meetings the House of Bishops and all the main central committees make decisions that affect the life of the Church. The members of most of the committees are democratically elected on a diocesan-wide basis and include clergy and lay people. In those days the same people, lay and clerical, tended to be the core members of most of these committees, to the point where it became incestuous, either because they were senior in their dioceses, they were dedicated committee people or they were ambitious, or any combination of the three. Some committee members were indeed elected for the professional skills they could contribute and many of them were glad to act as a service to the Church.

One of the bishops was chairman of each of the main councils and committees – a finger in every pie. The bishop who was chairman of the Adult Education Council, with which I was concerned, was an elderly and kindly avuncular man. He didn't seem to know a great deal about adult education and he consistently referred to one of the Council members, Marjorie McClatchie as Mrs McClatcherie, and the secretary, Margaret Larminie, he called Miss Laramie, as in 'The Man from …' The bishop was so concerned about being nice to everybody that sometimes he didn't know people's names or what was going on around him.

Father Liam Carey, the priest in charge of adult education in the Roman Catholic archdiocese of Dublin, was a member of the Council, and, from his vast experience in the field, gave us invaluable help in the early years of planning adult education in the Church of Ireland. One layman, who didn't seem to have to work for a living, served on most of the important central committees and worked almost full-time, unpaid, for the Church. He made a major contribution to the Church of Ireland over many years and was one of an inner group of power-brokers. He did, however, have at least one weakness: he was sometimes rude to bishops!

Church House, the building, was orderly, respectable and entirely devoid of character. There was no Christian symbol of any kind to be seen, not a plain cross, nor even a Celtic one. The absence of Christian symbols was often commented upon but I never heard why it was so. I could only assume that some extreme Protestant members of the Church might consider a cross 'Romish'. For some Northern Ireland members, where the majority of Church of Ireland people live, it was bad enough to have to come south to Dublin for meetings without having to face a cross in the hall of Church of Ireland House. Some other people would happily have had a crucifix. Even the freemasons have their symbol on their headquarters in Molesworth Street.

A day or two after I took up my appointment as Adult Education Officer I was sitting in my office in the college when there was a knock on the door. It was one of the bishops who was in the college on some other business and dropped in to wish me well in my new job. He sat down and talked a bit about the Church of Ireland and then said: 'You know the Church of Ireland treats her specialist officers badly.' He had held a non-parochial specialist post himself and was none too happy with the outcome. He didn't give me details and I wasn't sure what he meant at the time but I felt it was decent of him to let me know, as I wasn't well up in church politics. What I think he meant was that the constitution of the Church recognises only bishops and parochial clergy, therefore specialist officers were particularly vulnerable employment-wise. As it happened I worked two, three-year contracts as Adult Education Officer and left when I wanted to return to parish life without ever having been asked to sign a piece of paper.

I enjoyed my time in adult education. Amongst other things it gave me an interesting overview of the Church. Adult education did not receive wide approval in the Church of Ireland, it seems to me, because for most lay people Church membership is a simple belief in God expressed by commitment to the institution, affirmed through attendance at worship and for some, by involvement in its social life. The last thing that the average member wants to do is to be made to think about what they believe. They leave that to the clergy many of whom are not madly enthusiastic themselves about reflecting on their beliefs.

The attitude I encountered most in dealing with lay members of the Church over six years was their desire to affirm the Church of Ireland in contradistinction to the Roman Catholic Church. This was not, I believe, in any superior way but to counter something that was deep in the Protestant consciousness, largely from before the Second Vatican Council, the constantly repeated claim of the Roman Catholic Church to be the One True Church. All others who claimed to be Christians were in fact heretics – *extra ecclesiam non salus est* – outside the Church, meaning the Roman Catholic Church, there is no salvation. Protestants were particularly conscious of this in the south where the presence and influence of the Catholic Church was all pervasive and Church of Ireland people had a fear of being swamped. The Roman Catholic Church changed its mind on this issue at the Second Vatican Council and now allows that not only can other Christians be saved but that even people who are not Christians at all can, in certain circumstances, be saved. However Rome says that other Churches should be called 'ecclesial communities', as they are not Churches in the true sense of the word.

At the end of six years I missed the pastoral contact with people that one has in parishes and decided that, when a suitable parish became vacant, I would return to the parochial ministry. In the autumn of 1988 I was appointed to the parish of Donoughmore and Donard with Dunlavin in West Wicklow.

10

West Wicklow

The parish of Donoughmore and Donard with Dunlavin straddles the main road between Blessington and Baltinglass. The Donough-more and Donard end of the parish was mainly the Glen of Imaal stretching up to the foothills of Lugnaquilla, the highest peak in the Wicklow Mountains. Before I went there I knew of the Glen of Imaal only as the site of the army's artillery range. I knew that people had been killed and injured there by unexploded shells when they strayed into areas that were out of bounds to the public. I had also heard that the Glen was such a confined community geographically that there was inbreeding that resulted in lunacy.

Shortly after I arrived in the parish a parishioner told me that within each of the Catholic and Church of Ireland communities everybody was related to everybody else. So much so that a former parish priest told a new Church of Ireland rector on his arrival in the parish that everyone in the Glen was related except them-selves! It is true that there is an extensive web of interrelationship in the area but somehow they have managed to keep the gene pool healthy. Not only did I not discover lunacy, I discovered a com-munity of astute, able and intelligent farmers and country people whose families for generations had farmed the land successfully, so that most of them would live in the ear of the average city dweller and rent out the other.

I found that among Church of Ireland parishioners there was an above average attendance at church and a fierce loyalty to their parish. Many of these families lived their lives largely around the parish church and its social life. There were good relations with their Roman Catholic friends and neighbours, who were equally extensively inter-married, however there were remarkably few mixed marriages in the Glen. I'm not sure whether this was because they tended not to happen or, when they did, most of the couples moved away.

The other end of the parish was Dunlavin, which was geographically open and a somewhat less cohesive community with only one or two families related to each other. Parishioners, however, had no less commitment and loyalty to their parish. Numerically the Glen was the larger of the two former separate parishes that had recently come together. Again relations between the Church of Ireland and Roman Catholic communities in Dunlavin were good.

Hilary continued to work in the Theological College, travelling up and down the 30 odd miles each way to Rathgar, and Sarah and Ben became boarders at Wesley where they had been day-pupils while we lived in Dublin.

There is an inherent contradiction in the nature of the role of clergy in a parish. It is their responsibility to be leaders in worship and to help people grow in faith by learning more about Christianity and to develop in applying that faith to daily living in a world that is changing at an ever-increasing pace. However, the contradiction is that most ordinary Church members don't want to have to think, don't want to change themselves and don't want the Church to change. Change disturbs the secure refuge and place of escape from the ever-changing world that the Church has always been for them. The ideal is that the Church should be the place of retreat from the world where Christians are spiritually fed and re-charged in order to return to the world. The purpose is not only to survive in the world, but the better to contribute to it from Christian insights, and particularly from the spiritual nurture that worship ought to be.

As a new broom arriving in West Wicklow this is how I saw my work, and then I proceeded to spend most of my time during my first three years in the parish building new buildings and renovating old ones. This work took hundreds of hours of time on my own part and the part of parishioners at a cost of over £300,000. I suppose if we were entirely spiritual beings, like angels, we wouldn't need buildings, but then we wouldn't have many of the pleasures in life either. Whether we like it or not the Church needs buildings and it is better not to let them fall down, at least that was what I told myself.

I always found dealing with money in the context of the parish distasteful. I felt that soiling my smooth and scented priestly hands with filthy lucre was beneath me. To show how impossible it is for the clergy to win, I was criticised by some people because I never appealed for money, while others commended me for not asking for money because apparently one of my predecessors did so quite often. My attitude was that the parish belonged more to the parishioners than to me. They had lived there for years and their families had lived there for generations. I was a Johnnie-come-lately with a particular role and they and their children would be there long after I was gone. It was their parish and they knew what was needed in the way of money and it was up to them to provide it, and they did. It was the responsibility of the select vestries to raise and spend the money and the responsibility of the treasurers to look after the finances, and all of them in my time did it exceptionally well. One parish treasurer, an astute farmer, kept the parish accounts on the backs of used envelopes in his inside pocket but produced a fine set of accounts at the end of the year. He did something I had never seen before in a parish: he provided parallel columns showing the previous years accounts for comparison.

I did make one exception in handling parish money. There was one old gentleman who would give his annual subscription only into the hand of the rector himself. He didn't attend church so he couldn't put it on the plate and he wouldn't send it in to the treasurer. He would only give it to the rector. The treasurer used to tip me the wink a week or two before the sustentation account was due to close so that I could make one of my pastoral visits to Henry. Now Henry lived alone, almost entirely in the big flag-floored kitchen in the basement of his large, badly neglected house. There was a fire, with a heap of logs on the hearth complete with axe for chopping them on the spot. There was a scrubbed-top table that hadn't been scrubbed for years covered with the debris of unfinished meals, bottles and packets of medicines for a plethora of ailments. There were two chairs and a television. Henry was one of those farmers who came up the hard way and by dint of working all the hours that God gave over his long life he had a fine farm of land, and knew the value of money. However, he had little confidence in banks, and was particularly wary of those whose notice his business might attract if he kept all his money in one of them. He did have a bank account, but he kept a large amount of cash in the house.

I never had to remind Henry about his sustentation contribution. At some point during my visit he would remember it himself and give it to me. One year we were sitting in the kitchen talking when Henry interrupted the conversation and said: 'I must give you the sustentation.' He went upstairs and arrived back with what must have been the most modern thing in the house; a brand-new slim businessman's documents case with shiny brass locks. He cleared a space on the table and opened the case. Like bank robbers checking their booty in the old western films, the case was full to the brim with banknotes in piles of different denominations held together by elastic bands. It must have contained many thousands of pounds. Henry knew exactly how much he was to give me even though he had lost the envelope the treasurer had issued. He counted out the £270, handed it to me and closed the case. I put the money in my coat pocket and we continued our conversation. As I sat there I realised there was a fine wad of money in my pocket. I felt it carefully, took it out and said to Henry: 'I think you've given me too much money.' I put it out on the table and counted it. There was £2,700. Henry threw his head back and raised his arms in the air.

'O God, O God,' he said, distracted.

'It's all right,' I said, and calmed him down, and as the smallest denomination was £20, in order to save him further embarrassment I said as I handed him back the rest: 'I'll take £280, it'll make it easy.'

He suddenly became undistracted: 'You will not', he said, rooted in his pocket, took out a tenner and gave it to me and held his hand there for me to return a £20. I was embarrassed that he thought I was trying to extract more money from him, and was confirmed in my long-held view, to which I had made an exception for him, that I should have nothing to do with parish money.

By this time the effects of the Second Vatican Council had well and truly permeated the parishes. In Donoughmore, Donard and Dunlavin the two communities worked well together and Fr Kevin Lyon and I worked unselfconsciously together on matters that affected both communities. A recent development was that there was a number of Catholic children attending Donoughmore Church of Ireland school. This was as the result of parental choice, and Kevin never said what he thought of this development, other than to say it was a nuisance to have to make special arrangements for them to be prepared for first Holy Communion.

On the morning of a pastoral visit to the Catholic parish by Bishop Eamonn Walsh, the auxiliary bishop for the area, a parent of one of the Catholic children in Donoughmore School phoned me to ask if it would be possible to invite the bishop to visit the school. I told her that I would be happy to invite him and I would contact Father Lyon. I phoned Kevin and recounted the phone call from the parent and asked him if Bishop Walsh would come. As, however, there were two Church of Ireland schools in the parish, one in Dunlavin, I would have to ask him to visit both. The bishop hadn't arrived so Kevin agreed readily to ask him but, as the bishop had an extremely tight schedule, he wasn't sure he would be able to fit it in at short notice. He phoned back after a short while to say the bishop would be glad to visit both schools. The teachers were delighted and Bishop Walsh was excellent with the children and stayed in both of them much longer than I expected.

On a subsequent pastoral visit by Archbishop Caird to the Church of Ireland parish I invited Kevin to the rectory for coffee to meet him. Kevin, an exceptionally generous man, arrived with gifts for the Archbishop and for me and the two of them, both Gaeilgeóirí, talked together in Irish, about 10 per cent of which I understood. These events were important developments, building up acceptance and trust between two communities who in the not too distant past had maintained no more than a polite stand-off.

Around this time I received an invitation through Fr Cyprian Candon, editor of *Intercom*, the magazine that was read by nearly every priest and nun in the country, to give a paper on Adult Education in the Church of Ireland to the annual conference of the National Council of Priests. I arrived at the conference centre for lunch after which I went for a walk with the priest who was delegated to look after me until I spoke later in the afternoon. We talked of the difficulties of parochial ministry we had in common and he recounted the difficulties priests experienced in dealing with celibacy. He spoke graphically of the loneliness of returning home in the evening after a busy day in winter to a cold house with the ash in the fireplace from the previous night and having to turn around and make a meal. He told me that some priests missed the female dimension in their lives and had relationships of one kind or another with women. He himself had dinner out with a woman friend once a week. In due course my paper aroused a particular interest in how free Protestant lay people were to explore religious ideas for themselves if they had a mind to; they felt free to do their own theology; a phrase that formed the basis of a useful discussion.

In my West Wicklow parish, apart from parishioners, I came to know some interesting people who lived in the Glen. Jerome was in his sixties, a bachelor and shy; he survived beside the fire in his cottage on a few acres of land. He was something of a poet and had had a poem on the Glen of Imaal published in the local newspaper. I used to meet Jerome on the road wearing wellington boots and carrying a hessian bag, on his way to the local shop at Castleruddery and I always waved from the car, but Jerome would put his head down and walk on without a reck.

One Christmas at an old folk's party in Donoughmore Hall I saw Jerome standing on his own and I went over to talk to him.

'Hello, Jerome.'

'Hello,' he replied and took a half step backwards.

'Any more poems published?'

'No.' A silence.

'Do you enjoy occasions like this?' He looked at me with a

barely perceptible grin as if I was mad and then said simply: 'No.'

Since there was no chance Jerome would initiate a sentence, I asked him some more questions as the only way to keep the conversation going. He answered them all in no more than a word or two. Then I asked him: 'Is there anything that really annoys you?' There was a long silence I was determined not to fill. Slowly the hint of a smile crossed his lips.

'There is,' he said. I was making progress at last.

'What is it?' I asked.

'It's people asking me questions.'

Peter Kelly, a bachelor farmer, was another regular attendee of the annual Christmas party. I knew him from occasions when I stopped to talk at his gate when walking at Eadestown. Peter's farming was harmless. He was much more interested in repairing things that were broken, but didn't always get around to mending them. There was a Morris Minor car inside his gate that had grown old gracefully, and then slowly over the years slipped into dilapidation without further disturbance. Nearby there was a heap of lime that had not been touched since the day it was delivered some years before. Nature had covered it with a coating of grass and weeds as though to hide from the world her embarrassment at such waste.

Peter's great interest was astronomy. He would talk in unfinished sentences about the planets and the stars for as long as you had time to listen. He watched television, listened to the radio, and scoured newspapers to enhance his knowledge of the universe, and he wanted to share the awe he felt at its immensity and its mystery. His reason for not completing sentences seemed to me to be that he found the universe so incredible that if he stated fully the information he had gleaned from his sources, he believed it might stretch your credulity to the point you might question his reason. He would say only 'yes' to any comment you might interject for fear that anything more than that might deflect him from telling you more of his wonder at it all. He was for all the world like the man in Robert Frost's poem 'New Hampshire.'

'I knew a man who failing as a farmer
Burned down his farmhouse for the fire insurance,
And spent the proceeds on a telescope
To satisfy a lifelong curiosity
About our place among the infinities.
And how was that for other-worldliness?'

Peter and his abiding interest were a million miles away from the people who frequented the Gospel Hall at Ballyreaske in the Glen, where evangelical meetings were held from time to time. Some Church of Ireland parishioners attended them as well as attending the parish church, but none of them ever told me they did; they would have known, to say the least, that it wasn't my kind of religion. Nonetheless I accepted their right absolutely to attend where they liked for religious services and respected their right to hold different views to mine. What I was not prepared to do was to give my approval and the approval of the Church of Ireland parish, to anything that suggested that in order to be a real Christian a person had to have a certain kind of conversion experience. Some people hold the view that without a conversion experience a person isn't the 'full shilling' in the sight of God. This was the same kind of religion as the YMCA street preachers in Dublin in the 1950s.

One Sunday two men I didn't know arrived at the vestry in Donoughmore church before the morning service. They told me they were evangelical missionaries who were running a mission in the Gospel Hall during the coming week and would I be kind enough to announce it at the service. I explained to them that I didn't feel I could announce it but I would talk about it in my sermon. The two men attended the service and sat towards the back of the church, and when it came to the sermon I said they were welcome, as any stranger was welcome, to join in our worship, and I said who they were and what they had asked me to do.

I told the congregation that anybody was free to attend the mission in the hall and I would not want to interfere with that freedom, but I felt in conscience bound to tell people how I regarded such a mission. If it was a matter of saying some prayers and singing hymns it wouldn't do anyone any harm. If it was a case that those who led the mission thought that being a member of the Church of Ireland wasn't enough and in order to be a 'real' Christian something more in the way of a conversion experience was necessary I could not support it. I have no idea who, if anyone, from the parish went to the mission and I never heard a word about how it turned out. I believe it is wrong of anybody to claim that others are not 'real' Christians in this way; however, many people hold this kind of view.

On one occasion a family in the parish, for whom I had the greatest respect, asked me to announce in church a mid-week afternoon gospel hymn singing for small children in their home. Somebody from Dublin was coming down with a guitar to lead it. The family willingly gave me more details when I asked, and I concluded that there was a possibility that the person from Dublin might conduct a children's evangelical meeting of the kind that could become emotionally charged, and be in danger of becoming manipulative of small children. I explained this and said I could not give it official approval by announcing it in church. However I agreed that as I could not be sure as to its nature I would not express my opinion unless I was asked, as they were entitled to invite to their home anybody they liked.

The family were good people and exceptionally loyal parishioners, and I'm not sure if they understood. I was particularly cautious where children were concerned. I had had a first-hand account of a children's weekend away run by an evangelical group where children had nightmares and got out of bed during the night in a highly-charged emotional state, trying to get out of the dormitory to escape from the devil. A rector of a different theological hue might have taken a different position on the Gospel Hall mission and the children's singing group.

During parish discussion groups held during Lent and at other times, people expressed all kinds of opinions and this was a good thing. It was inevitable that my own liberal or even radical position would come up for discussion, though I didn't push it. Rather I outlined it for people to consider. In essence it was that our belief in God through Jesus Christ was traditionally couched in forms of thinking dating from the first four or five centuries. Today, with two thousand years of development of human experience and learning behind us, it might be helpful to express what we believe in a twentieth century way. Doing this made Christianity more credible to me and I though it might help some other people to do the same.

In fact this was the case. Some people, but by no means all, found the expression of Christianity in a twentieth century form of thinking a revelation and a release. Some of them had been struggling secretly for years with questions and doubts about their faith since traditional expressions of the faith did not satisfy them. Hearing a clergyman struggling with the same kinds of issues was a relief to them, and gave them licence to be open and express their own particular questions and to begin to work with them. In fact a number of them took the Archbishop's Diploma in Theology over two years, part-time, and ended up knowing almost as much theology as the rector.

The tension between different theological positions within Anglicanism is ever present in the Church of Ireland. They are part of its strength, in that it allows for diversity and meets the needs of different kinds of people. It is also part of its weakness, in that it makes it difficult for the Church to speak with one voice on some issues and creates a problem of authority for some people, however none of us has the right to try to put God in our own pocket.

Because of theological difference, differences of personality and differing gifts and priorities, any one rector cannot be congenial to all parishioners. In my view it is important that clergy do not stay too long in a parish in order that the next rector, who will inevitably be different, may meet the needs of and be more acceptable to parishioners whom his/her predecessor did not suit. Furthermore a rector who stays too long in a parish is in danger of becoming stale and the fresh approach of a new one can renew a community.

After eight years in West Wicklow I felt I had run my course and needed a change. Around this time there was to be a change of Archbishop, so I spoke to the Archdeacon who suggested that I consider the Parish of St George and St Thomas, Cathal Brugha Street, Dublin, which was soon to be vacant. It included the chaplaincies to three hospitals and Mountjoy Prison. It would certainly be a contrast to anything I had ever done before and after discussion of the pros and cons with Hilary I decided to make the move.

11

The Chaplaincies

I left a parish in the heart of scenic Wicklow countryside, peopled mainly by farmers and with three churches, two schools, two parish halls and over 400 parishioners, a good proportion of whom were young people. I exchanged it for a parish in the north inner city of Dublin with one church, St George and St Thomas, off O'Connell Street in the centre of the city, no schools, no halls and about thirty-five parishioners, only one or two of whom was under fifty years of age. The contrast could not have been greater, but then contrasts add spice to life and this was what I wanted.

You are probably thinking that this was little more than a sinecure. Before you rush to judgement you must take account of the fact that within the parish there were three major hospitals, the Mater Public, Mater Private and Temple Street Children's Hospital and the country's largest prison, Mountjoy. As chaplain to these four institutions, in addition to the parish, I had, for me, more than a full-time job.

The parish of St George and St Thomas was the remnant of a former large parish on the north side of the city. The parish inevitably diminished as the centre of the city declined and people moved out to the suburbs. The remaining small group of parishioners made up in enthusiasm and loyalty what they lacked in numbers. They had a terrific pride in their parish and a determination to survive. Towards the end of my time in that parish, parishioners gave a warm welcome to some refugees and asylum seekers who began attending Sunday morning services. There was a welcome for the stranger that is sometimes absent in more populous and affluent parishes.

I know that many of my clerical colleagues, while perhaps not going as far as 'sinecure', saw the parish of St George and St Thomas as light duty. It could have been light duty if it had not been for the hospital and prison chaplaincies. I became involved in these not only with patients and prisoners, but with my fellow chaplains and chaplaincy organisations. I could not speak highly enough of the support I received from my Catholic chaplain colleagues and from the management of the hospitals and the prison.

Every member of the parish clergy does a certain amount of visiting their sick parishioners at home and in hospital. Parish clergy also give sacramental and pastoral care at home to parishioners approaching death and to bereaved families. Hospital chaplaincy, which is a matter of doing this almost full-time is a different kettle of fish. I never had any serious difficulty visiting the sick but I did feel some stress and nervousness coping with death and bereavement. A rector, in whose parish I conducted a funeral once, flummoxed me by commenting on what I considered my normal nervousness in the vestry before the service. He remarked, 'Conducting a funeral doesn't take a thing out of me.' Horses for courses.

I wasn't entirely sure how I was going to feel about being a hospital chaplain until I started the job. Although I had thirty years experience in the ministry, I did not have the standard qualification for hospital chaplains – Clinical Pastoral Education. CPE is a training for people working in pastoral care, which is particularly suitable for hospital chaplaincy. Its distinctiveness lies in that it approaches theological problems primarily through human experience rather than through book learning. Students bring the practical experience of ministering back to their study group for sharing and reflection. They do this in such a way as to integrate their theology with their ministry, increase their understanding of themselves as they minister and increase their understanding of the needs of those to whom they minister. Boison, the founder of CPE, saw it as looking at 'the living human document'. With the supervision of the director of the programme the student is helped to a greater self-assurance and effectiveness.

I know I would have benefited greatly from doing even one unit of CPE, but with my work commitments I did not have time and furthermore I was approaching the upper age limit for starting. I did however have fulsome support from some of the finest people one could work with: the priests, nuns, and laywomen who were Catholic chaplains at the Mater Hospital. During this time I tried to heighten the awareness of Church of Ireland chaplains in the Diocese of Dublin to the value of CPE and to encourage them to pursue it. Furthermore, Angela, the determined human resources manager of the Mater Private Hospital used her wiles to rope me into extra-curricular activities such as staff inductions that gave me a broader view of hospital life.

Whereas parish clergy visit the sick and minister to the bereaved, this is with parishioners they know. Hospital chaplains, on the other hand, minister to patients and families about whom they know little. Every new patient is a stranger in hospital for anything from personal matters like adult circumcision or breast reduction to terminal cancer, open-heart surgery or heart transplant. I even had patients in hospital for cosmetic surgery; one woman treated herself every now and again to some nip or tuck instead of an annual holiday in the sun. Some patients are in for a day or two, some for weeks and some never go home. The length of stay in these days of bed shortages is as short as possible.

Some patients are involved in their home parishes and are usually glad to see you. A chaplain often hears unsolicited comments about some of his colleagues, as a home rector becomes a likely topic for a patient to introduce. When I heard praise of home rectors I smiled and approved, and when I heard criticism I remained impassive and silent and tucked the gossip away in the back of my mind never to be retrieved. Some patients have no connection with Church at all but some of these are glad of your visit and will ask you to come back, while some, though usually polite, don't want to know. I approached one patient who was lying down with my usual spiel: 'Hello, my name is Patrick Semple, I'm the Church of Ireland chaplain.' With a look of utter disdain she pulled the bedclothes up around her and without uttering a word turned her back to me. As

I left, smiling to myself, the patient in the next bed looked at me strangely as though I had offended her neighbour.

On one occasion nurses called me at home in the middle of the night when a patient I had seen that afternoon had died. I dressed and went in but discovered there was no family there to be comforted. In future I was careful to ask the circumstances when called at night. Some nurses seemed to have the impression that there was some formula to be administered as soon after death as possible. As far as the Church of Ireland is concerned there isn't. As far as I was concerned prayers are for the sick and dying and for relatives.

I was once with a wife, her adult son and a nun beside the bed of an old man dying in a provincial hospital. As we kept vigil the nun, from her nursing experience, saw that the patient was about to expire. She grabbed me and pulled me down onto my knees and said, 'He's going. Pray!' I didn't. I'm not sure why I should pray then when I had already said prayers when I arrived. I'm not sure either what in particular I was to pray about. Perhaps it was that the good sister believed that if prayers were being said at the moment of his departure he had a better chance of going up than down. I do not believe that. Years later I asked a priest friend about it and he said something non-committal about prayers always being a help, but I didn't question him further. I suppose it is because death is such a dramatic and final event people feel they want to counter it with prayer. Death in my experience is always traumatic, even with old people and in bed, so I cannot understand the current fashion for using a reading at funerals from Scott Holland that begins: 'Death is nothing at all …' It damned well is. When there is a family to suffer the loss and to grieve for months and sometimes years, or a widow for whom life will never be the same again, how can anyone say death is nothing at all? It may be comforting to say at a funeral, but it's not true.

Talking of dying in bed reminds me of a story a parishioner in Stradbally told me. Willie was an old soldier in his eighties. He and three brothers had joined up for the First World War. Willie was the only one that survived. After one fierce battle his unit was retreating when he saw a wounded soldier lying in a ditch beckoning to him.

Willie went over and the soldier asked him to unlace and take off his boots. As he did so Willie asked him had his feet swollen.

'No,' said the wounded man, 'my father always told me I'd die with my boots on.'

What does a chaplain bring when he/she visits a patient in hospital? My understanding is that the chaplain is bringing love; unconditional love as we know it in Jesus. A chaplain also brings support for whatever spiritual resources the patient has. It is not a case of simply dispensing a formula or a ritual, but of being available to offer love and support. Even for people about to die I could never volunteer assurance about the afterlife because I didn't believe in it myself. The Church teaches that there is life after death, but as to its nature and timing there is no consistency. A parishioner of mine once recounted to me that when her widowed father was about to die, his local rector, at the bedside with the family, said: 'John it's all right to let go, Mary is on the other side waiting to welcome you.'

My parishioner looked at me and said: 'I don't believe that kind of thing, do you?'

'No,' I replied, 'I don't. "Don't be afraid to let go," yes, but not the rest.'

It is human for people to want to survive death in some shape or form and to hope for eternal bliss. In my time in the ministry I met maybe ten or twelve people that I knew of who went to church regularly and told me that they did not believe in life after death. These included one woman in her eighties who would never miss church on a Sunday. This issue was the beginning of my own serious questioning of the whole edifice of the Christian faith.

As a hospital chaplain it was a great privilege, despite my own inadequacies and uncertainties, to be present with patients and their families in extremis, and with families in bereavement. One's presence and care are appreciated and often, within reason, the less you say the better. To be sensitive to their needs and what is appropriate for them is what's important. The most tragic situation I encountered in my time as a hospital chaplain was a woman who died after a short illness. I had visited her a few times, but she was, to say the least, not forthcoming. When she died the social worker discovered there were no relatives. Nobody, other than a staff member from the old people's home from which she was admitted, had visited her while she was in hospital. Nobody had been to see her while she was in the home either and they knew of no relatives. I arranged the funeral and the hospital social worker, Margaret, and I were the only mourners as the cemetery attendants lowered her coffin into the cold earth in the pauper's plot in Glasnevin Cemetery.

As we walked away I mused upon a life that should have come to such an end. She was a baby once, with smiles and laughter that lifted hearts and whose first steps gave joy. As a child she donned her first schoolbag with excitement. As a young girl she giggled and no doubt shared secrets with her friend. As a teenager she'd have thrilled at the first notice by a boy. Probably as an adult she felt pride in earning her first wage. These things I could speculate, but what joys and pains the following sixty or more years held I could not surmise. Nobody deserves such an ending: over eighty years of life brought to a close with two strangers at the graveside and a wreath from the local authority.

Mountjoy Prison, by its very nature, is an inhospitable place. The same could not be said of those who run it. The Governor, John Lonergan, and the Chief Officer, Jim Petherbridge, and their staff could not have been more helpful to their new Church of Ireland chaplain as I came to terms with what must be one of the strangest environments in which clergy work. The Chief Officer brought me on a tour of the prison and introduced me to people in charge – the Medical Unit, the Separation Unit, St Patrick's for young offenders and the Female Prison.

It took me months to get the hang of things and to work out a routine. People are not always where you expect to find them in a prison so a routine is always provisional. Mr Duffy, an assistant governor, was the one I went to most often when I needed to know the lie of the land. I learned most about prisoners from review boards, chaired by an official from the prisons' section of the Department of Justice. The board consisted of an assistant governor, a senior officer, a social worker and a chaplain all of whom had daily dealings with the prisoner under review. Each was encouraged to have their say on whether the prisoner in question should be granted whatever leave or concession he had applied for. I heard the experienced professionals assessing and evaluating and making carefully considered recommendations to the official from the Department. The whole process was conducted thoroughly and gave me great insights into the treatment of prisoners. It also gave me confidence in the fairness of the system.

I visited the prison two days a week. My Catholic chaplain colleagues spent five or six days a week, nine o'clock to five and often much more, in the oppressive atmosphere helping prisoners through problem after problem, especially crises concerning wives and children at home. They were always ready to help and support their neophyte Church of Ireland part-time colleague. Like my friends in hospital chaplaincy they were a fine group of people, priests and nuns, committed to serving the prisoners without judgment and without fear or favour, and they did all with a sense of humour that lightened the load.

When Catholic prisoners asked to attend the Church of Ireland chapel on a Sunday morning, usually out of curiosity, or for the opportunity to meet female prisoners, since there was a separate Mass for Catholic females, at first I used to let one of the Catholic chaplains know. Soon one of them told me there was no need to mention it since if they didn't go to the Church of Ireland service they probably wouldn't go to Mass anyway. One Church of Ireland prisoner went every Sunday to Mass because, fancying himself as a singer, he had the opportunity to sing for an audience. At one Good Friday service while I was reading the long gospel account of the arrest, trial and crucifixion of Jesus I noticed one of the prisoners looking and listening intently. He was mesmerised. I could see that he was no longer in that prison chapel, but in the garden at the arrest, in the *praetorium* at the trial and on the Hill of Calvary at the crucifixion. It was probably the first time that he had heard the story in sequence or perhaps at all. I was sorry when he was not in chapel on Easter Sunday to hear the *dénouement*.

The prisoners I felt particularly sorry for were the young men and women drug couriers arrested while bringing drugs into the country. Many of them didn't use drugs themselves but were seduced by substantial sums of money into transporting them for dealers who couldn't care less when they were caught. There were young people in for other crimes most of whom came from socially deprived families or from broken homes. The only person in touch with one young prisoner was one of his grandmothers, who knew what appalling things he had had to endure as a child and was determined, despite all, to support him as best she could. One young gay man was serving a sentence for an assault as he tried to protect himself from the sexual advances of an older man. He was a remarkably sensitive and good-humoured person who found prison difficult, but coped with cheerfulness and courage.

My first meeting with one young prisoner convinced me that he was deeply depressed and I feared he might be suicidal. I told this to a chief officer who arranged immediately to have him put into a strip-cell ostensibly for his own safety. I felt really badly about this. In a strip-cell a prisoner wears only his underpants and in the cell there is only a mattress on the floor and a blanket of such material the prisoner could not use it to harm himself. He would have to stay there until a psychiatrist could see him and that could be in two, three or maybe four days' time. This is a barbaric and uncivilised thing for the State to do to a sick man. This was not the fault of the prison staff but of the Department of Justice and ultimately the government who provided woefully inadequate psychiatric services to the prison. Politicians in power, largely speaking, don't care about people, especially prisoners. They care about power and where the votes will come from to keep them where they are. The old tag is true: 'there are no votes in prison reform'.

The main concern of the prison understandably was for security and containment. There was negligible rehabilitation or therapy. Considering the size of the drug problem amongst prisoners, drug rehabilitation programmes barely scratched the surface. The Quakers run an excellent voluntary programme in the prison at weekends. This is the Alternative to Violence Programme, run on group learning principles where prisoners after a certain stage can themselves become members of the training team. I recommended to a number of prisoners that they should take the programme. When I asked one prisoner what he learned at the weekend at one of these courses he said with amazement, 'I learned that there are ways to get children to do what you want without hitting them.'

Willie Bridcut, the Church of Ireland chaplain at Arbor Hill Prison and I were always invited to the Catholic prison chaplain training courses and annual conferences. At one conference on the Friday night the conference opened with a Mass in the convent chapel where it was held. Willie and I took part in the Mass and the whole group of ten or twelve of us administered communion to each other standing in a circle at the altar. There was a great feeling of oneness, as there is on such occasions, and I know the Catholic chaplains, to a person, were delighted that we communicated and took full part. We worked together during the year without inhibition and we worshipped together on this occasion in the same way.

Bishop Eamonn Walsh, the Catholic bishop responsible for prison chaplaincy, was coming to celebrate the Mass on Saturday morning. He was the bishop who had taken the trouble to adjust his schedule to visit the Church of Ireland schools in the parish in West Wicklow. I asked one of the priest chaplains who was to meet the bishop when he arrived to confirm that it was all right for Willie and me to communicate. He said that of course it was all right. However, I insisted he ask the bishop and he did. He came into the chapel before the service embarrassed and said the bishop had been firm in saying 'no'. The chaplain was most apologetic. Willie and I, though disappointed, brushed it off and said we understood it was different for a bishop and that was why we had asked.

When it came to the communion the rest of the chaplains went forward and formed a circle around the altar to receive. Willie and I stayed in our pews. When some of the others, who didn't know what had transpired, saw we weren't coming forward they beckoned us to join them and we demurred as discreetly as we could. When the bishop had communicated the others he came down to us and greeting us warmly said: 'I'm sorry, I just couldn't.' We wanted to put him at his ease and said it was all right, that we perfectly understood his position.

After the Mass the priest chaplain who had spoken to the bishop before the Mass explained to the others what had happened. They were furious. I thought that four of the sisters would devour the bishop before breakfast. They saw no reason in the circumstances of a small group in a private chapel why the spirit of the law could not prevail over the letter. I helped to calm them down by saying that it was our fault as we had put the man in the awkward situation. In my experience there is a division amongst Catholic priests on this matter, some holding the position of the chaplains on the Friday night would give communion to non-Roman Catholics in this circumstance, and others, holding the position of the Bishop on the Saturday morning, would not.

This incident was in contrast with an occasion around the same time when at a funeral Mass a Catholic bishop gave communion to the local Church of Ireland rector whom he knew personally. The rector was robed and in the sanctuary with the other priests, but the bishop could quite easily have passed him by. This was in front of a full church at the funeral of a notable member of the local community. The Christian love created by such an act helps to break down barriers and build trust between two parts of the broken body of Christ, both struggling to be faithful to His gospel of love. Such an act can only bring about much good in contrast to the division that is reinforced by the withholding of communion from members of a tradition with a somewhat different understanding of the eucharist. I wonder what Jesus would have done in these two situations? The Roman Catholic Church does allow Anglicans travelling abroad to receive communion in a Catholic Church where there is no Anglican church within reach.

The whole of humanity and the whole of society are represented in prison, but not in fair proportions. The prison population is heavily weighted in the direction of young men in their teens and twenties from socially deprived areas of cities. There are people in prison that should still be there into old age and never freed; people who have committed the most appalling crimes and are likely to reoffend. There are people in prison who should never be there in the first place; people who have defaulted on fines and who have committed petty crimes, not against the person, and there are people in prison who have committed crimes that range anywhere between these two extremes.

Who could live in Ireland these days and not believe that there are people who should serve long sentences who will never end up in prison? Businessmen, politicians and other wealthy tax criminals. There is undoubtedly one law for the rich and another for the poor. A prisoner once held a newspaper up to me with a headline about the financial affairs of a senior politician and asked me what he himself was doing in prison for a £150 cheque fraud when the politician was outside living in luxury. I told him I agreed with him entirely. Most politicians have no motivation when it comes to the need to correct this imbalance and perhaps some of them are afraid that if they change things they themselves or their colleagues may end up on the wrong side of the law. In my view politicians should not have ultimate control of the penal justice system. Some way should be devised whereby an impartial group of human beings who understand the issues of people and power should have the say in controlling justice and in determining penalties. Central to this would be the removal of the imbalance between rich man's crime and poor man's crime and to give a greater emphasis to rehabilitation than to retribution. Some chance.

I never met a prisoner who claimed to be innocent of the crime for which he was in prison. Neither did I ever meet a prisoner that believed his sentence was too lenient, but I did encounter a number who believed their sentences were too harsh. One middle-aged man was sentenced to three years for possession of cannabis. He smoked a joint or two on Friday nights with some friends. His appeal against the severity of sentence came up for hearing after he had spent about a year in prison. It succeeded and he was released from the Appeal Court, showing how well, at least on this occasion, the appeal system works.

In my experience the prison regime at Mountjoy was fair and humane. The example was set by the governor and seemed to me to permeate to most officers in their dealings with prisoners. There were some exceptional incidents, but they were exceptional. When things were running normally officers and prisoners interacted easily, but if prisoners cut up rough, officers were capable of cutting up rough too and they were well-trained and able to deal with difficult situations.

Of course there is pain and tragedy in any prison. What it is like to be a prisoner I do not know, I can hardly imagine, but the atmosphere in the small female prison at Mountjoy was particularly relaxed. One hot summer day I found a female prisoner I wanted to see out in the exercise yard playing netball. We spoke for a while and as I was leaving, Eamon, one of my chaplain colleagues called me from the far end of the yard where he was surrounded by a small group of prisoners.

'Pat, what would you say to these ladies, they're calling me a paedophile?' Eamon was taking it all in good part, and before I had time to say anything one of the women shot the question at me: 'Who are you?'

'I'm the Church of Ireland chaplain.'

'A Protestant', she said in mock horror and stood back a few paces, put up her fists and started to shadow box me. Suddenly she aimed a real punch at my crotch. Fortunately she missed, but Eamon was covered with embarrassment, and I never answered his question. On my way down the yard I passed two young women: 'Howya Father?'

'How are things girls?' And like a shot out of a gun one of them came back: 'Nothing a big black pint wouldn't cure, Father.' Humour in prison is a contribution towards survival.

After approximately three years back in Dublin I retired from the active ministry. I'm not sure what the inactive ministry is, but that is how Church of Ireland clergy who retire describe it, and that is how I describe it in order not to be different.

Over thirty-two years I met hundreds if not thousands of fascinating people the likes of whom I would not have met if I had continued to work in insurance, not that that was why I left. Even boring people are interesting if you can stay awake long enough, which in fact I failed to do on a number of occasions while making parish calls. The first time I failed to stay awake on a visit I was sitting beside a hot cooker in a farmer's small stuffy kitchen after lunch, on a wet winter afternoon with outdoor clothes drying on the rack over the cooker. The parishioner, an old man, sent me to sleep as he rambled on about the technicalities of ploughing with horses in the old days. When I woke, so absorbed was he in his subject, he was still talking and hadn't noticed my temporary absence. On the other occasions when it happened I wasn't so lucky and I don't know whether the parishioner in each case or I was the more embarrassed. One tried to put me at my ease by saying she understood how hard I worked!

During my time in the ministry my understanding of and belief in the Christian faith evolved. I believe that if a person believes today exactly what they believed ten or twenty years ago it is not healthy and even then conclusions are always provisional. People of faith should, I believe, constantly test their faith against their life experience and grow and develop in their understanding of God and the world in which they live.

My problem was that I could not stop my head working as I tried to reconcile my understanding of the world, the universe and the whole cabush, with what I believed about Christianity. I could not reconcile them.

I was brought up in the tiny Protestant minority in the south of Ireland, in the shadow of the 95 per cent majority Roman Catholic Church which, when I was a child, controlled tightly the lives of its members and virtually the State itself. I would now like to show more particularly how, as I grew up, the Roman Catholic Church and its beliefs and practices appeared to members of the minority Church of Ireland community in the south of Ireland. I will also say something about how I see the relationship of the itinerant preacher from Nazareth with the institutional Church of the twenty-first century, and finally I will say something about my present understanding of the Christian faith, what I believe and what I don't believe.

12

Looking On

In the previous chapters I gave some account of how Roman Catholicism in Ireland appears to Protestants, particularly to the tiny minority of Protestants in the south of Ireland. I now want to deal with the matter of differences more specifically. I can only speak for myself but I believe that most of what I say will be reasonably representative of how Protestants in general see the Catholic Church. That Church of course appears, in many ways, very differently today in the early years of the twenty-first century from how it appeared in the 1940s and 1950s, a span of only fifty or sixty years. As a parishioner once put it to me: 'As far as Catholics are concerned one day we Protestants were all going to hell and the next they're singing our hymns.'

Above all, as far as it lies within me, I want to say what I have to say, in a non-partisan way and as objectively as possible. I hope I can be without prejudice, but no doubt it is not possible for me to be entirely objective. My perspective will inevitably betray some lack of objectivity of which I am not conscious and if this is pointed out to me I will be glad to acknowledge it. The danger in recounting how Protestants see Roman Catholicism is that the popular Protestant view may be false or even half true which is worse. I pointed out the problem of half-truths the other way around, when Catholics talk about their understanding of the Protestant position on Henry VIII and belief in the Virgin Mary.

The picture I want to paint is primarily of how the average lay Protestant sees the Catholic Church in day-to-day terms, but since there is a diversity within Protestantism this may be difficult to achieve. While aware that the way Protestants see Roman

Catholicism is not always how Roman Catholicism actually is, setting out the Protestant perspective may help to clear the air for some and may even be a minor contribution to practical ecumenism. It may, however, sometimes be difficult for me to give the layperson's view since I have had a theological training and I am bound to understand and say things from that perspective.

It is inevitable that a Protestant perspective on Catholicism will, in the nature of things, be critical, as would be a Catholic perspective on Protestantism. There is a virtual universal human response that says that I may be as critical as I like of my own family or of my own tribe, but I resent and will resist criticism of it by anybody from outside. A Catholic telling a joke about Catholicism or a Protestant telling a joke about Protestantism is one thing, but either telling a joke about the other's religion has a different perspective, and something of an edge. There are all kinds of feelings of tribal and religious loyalty deep in the gut of most people irrespective of the rights and wrongs of the matter. I want to say to readers that if anything I say is offensive to them no offence is intended.

A Catholic friend once told me the joke about St Peter showing a new arrival around heaven and saying 'shhh' and tiptoeing past one particular door. On being asked why, St Peter replied, 'That's where all the Roman Catholics are and they think they're the only ones here.' This coming from a Catholic, as it did, is one thing, but if a Protestant tells the same joke, especially to Catholics it has a different complexion. This joke about St Peter passing the door in heaven quietly, however, could just as readily be told about evangelical Protestants as about Catholics, as some evangelical Protestants too claim to know the mind of God and believe they have exclusive access to heaven. The brand of broad church Anglicanism in which I was brought up tends not to make these kinds of judgements. It is vague, and some would say wishy-washy on the subject, and if challenged would probably say this is a matter better left to God despite what Pope or Protestant preacher may say. Conservative Catholicism and evangelical Protestantism paradoxically have much in common.

Over the years a favourite theme of mine was the injunction of Jesus, 'judge not that you be not judged'. I believe firmly that there is nothing, but nothing, that I can accuse another person of but that I am guilty of it, in some shape or form, myself – even murder. Did Jesus not say that to have malice in your heart for someone is to have committed murder already and I have often had malicious thoughts, and the same for adultery – you can do it in your heart, and I have often done that too. I believe the same of any judgement I may make of Roman Catholicism; in some shape or form Protestantism is subject to the same judgement. For example Catholic belief in the infallibility of the Pope and Protestant belief in the infallibility of the Church or of the Bible are much the same in intent: to prove the incontrovertibility of what is taught and in my view all are equally unsustainable.

The only comment made about Roman Catholics I remember as a child, in my home or in school, was positive. It was my mother commending Catholics for their assiduous observance of their religious duties. I don't remember, but I have no doubt that this comment was in contrast with attendance at church in the Church of Ireland parish that would have been noticeably more casual. As I grew up I realised that Roman Catholic children claimed to know more about Protestants than I knew about Roman Catholics. They informed me of matters about Protestants of which I was not aware, and in fact, as it transpired, were not always true. It seems they were taught in school about how Protestantism differed from Roman Catholicism and that it was faulty or deficient, and in my experience there was no equivalent teaching or even mention about Roman Catholicism in Protestant schools. One day when our daughter Sarah was about ten or eleven she asked Hilary: 'Are we Catholics or Protestants?'

In the Church of Ireland parish of Wexford there was a rector, and from time to time when the parish could afford one, a curate. I saw around the town a variety of Catholic religious: priests, friars, brothers, and nuns, and there seemed to me to be a lot of them. It took me a while before I could figure out where they all belonged; priests in the parish and St Peter's College, and the brothers and nuns running schools. I soon learned to distinguish brothers from priests by their half collars. I gleaned from my Catholic friends that the brothers were tough customers who imposed iron discipline in their school. I had the impression that they could be, to say the least, severe on boys who stepped out of line in the way of discipline or didn't measure up in the way of learning. I had the impression that priests were also feared, not from wielding the strap, but from, as I would put it as an adult, the awesome power they had over people's immortal souls. The nuns dealt with girls and I didn't know much about them, while the friars in their brown habits and sandals seemed to be the most human of them all.

It seemed that for my Catholic friends religion was ever present; it permeated the whole of their lives. The public face of the Catholic religion was the presence of so many priests and nuns and by people blessing themselves passing churches, at the Angelus, during sport and when they heard bad news or bad language. I was aware of Roman Catholicism when people went in large numbers to retreats, sodalities and to the churches on holy days and during Lent, not to mention Sundays when the whole town turned out to Mass. There were three Catholic churches in the town and there were religious statues outside churches, convents and schools. All of these things were part of a different life from mine. I was conscious that my family and the Church of Ireland community to which I belonged functioned religiously in a somewhat lower key.

Whereas Protestants were aware that there was a variety of Protestant denominations, they saw the Roman Catholic Church as a single uniform monolith, tightly controlled by rules enforced by an authoritarian clergy. They understood why Catholic children were taught the teachings of the Church at an early age, aware of the belief of the Jesuits that if they had access to a child until he or she was seven, that person would always be a Catholic. My own religious education, as a middle-of-the-road Anglican, was learning Bible stories, hymns and the catechism. I should 'do unto all men as I would they should do unto me, to hurt nobody by word or deed: to be true and just in all my dealings: to bear no malice or hatred in my heart: to keep my hands from picking and stealing and my tongue from evil speaking, lying and slandering: to keep my body in temperance, soberness and chastity.' I have no doubt that in substance Catholic children were taught the same, but when they failed they had to go to the priest to confess and be forgiven. I was taught that God would forgive me if I were genuinely sorry and told him so.

Religious duties for Catholics seem to be compulsory on pain of sin. As I understand it for Catholics sin is not only a matter of contravention of the moral law, to steal, to lie, to commit adultery and so on, but it is a grave sin to contravene a church law, for example not to attend Mass on Sunday. The former are also sins for Protestants, but whether you go to church on Sunday is, to put it simply, a matter for yourself and your conscience. The division of sins into venial and mortal is a distinction not made in my religious tradition. I was taught that something was either right or wrong, and if you did something that was wrong you should be sorry and confess it to God who would forgive you. Though there is a general confession in the services of the Church, you could confess anywhere you liked; as you walked along the street, in your room, anywhere, and there was no need to involve the clergy or anybody else; it was a matter between you and God.

Most Protestants would find it unacceptable to have compulsory confession through a priest. It is the most intimate possible verbal communication, although there is the provision in Anglicanism to do so voluntarily in the case of grave sin should a penitent want to. Especially difficult would be recounting one's sexual thoughts. Everybody has them, even Popes and Archbishops have them, clergy of all denominations have them, as do men and women of every theological hue. They are I believe, in moderation nothing more than a natural device to keep sex alive so that people who love each other can express their love and at the same time contribute towards the survival of the species. On the other hand I suppose there are fantasies and fantasies, sexual sins and sexual sins. It seems to Protestants that Roman Catholicism is over anxious about sex and sexual sins, and Protestants find the idea of compulsory celibacy difficult to accept. Most Protestants would have no difficulty with celibacy voluntarily chosen. Despite what celibate priests say about understanding family life because they were brought up in a family, they simply cannot understand the complexities of a conjugal relationship, or of a paternal relationship unless they have themselves been husband or father.

There is a sin/guilt cycle that says that if you inculcate children early in life with enough guilt for sin, and if you control the means of expiating that guilt through religious ritual, you then have control of that person. This, I believe, is what the Jesuits meant, and I believe this is confirmed by the insights of modern psychology. The same sin/guilt cycle is evident in some manifestations of right-wing Protestantism. Children's missions consist of inculcating very young children with a strong sense of sin and guilt and then holding out the opportunity of salvation by inducing a certain kind of emotional conversion experience. This sequence is then reinforced during the life of the adult by repeating the process.

I know a man who was brought up in a conservative evangelical Protestant group who in adulthood abandoned it and now doesn't practise any religion. It seems to me he betrays a niggling doubt that there might be something in this sin/guilt cycle. He hasn't been able to abandon it without some residual guilt. On an evening out with some Catholic friends of many years we discussed religion and one of them said: 'The thing I like about you Protestants is that you're not wracked with guilt.' I had to put her straight and point out to her the diversity within Protestantism. Some Protestants are wracked with guilt, but in the middle-of-the-road Anglicanism to which I belong there is generally a healthy guilt that functions as guilt should to remind one of having done something wrong and to do something about it. It doesn't lead to an obsessive sense of unease with one's humanity and an unhealthy preoccupation with sin that can become an unhealthy preoccupation with religion.

It seems that Roman Catholicism seeks to keep a tight control on its members and has an extensive catechism and canon law for achieving it, while for instance Anglicanism has a simple catechism and keeps canon law to a minimum. Until relatively recently the Catholic Church determined by an Index that Catholics could not read certain books that the Church thought might adversely affect their faith or morals. Pope John Paul II told Catholics they were not even to discuss the ordination of women. At the Council of Chalcedon, AD 451, the Church fathers, believing they had solved the controversial issues concerning the divinity of Christ decreed: '… that no one is permitted to produce or even write down or compose any other creed or to think or teach otherwise.'

So there is precedent for the Pope's recent prohibition against discussing, or even thinking about the ordination of women, but this is alien to Protestants who would not brook anybody telling them what they could or could not read or discuss. They would make up their own minds. It seems that these prohibitions are primarily about the institutional Church's power to exercise control over its members. The experience of the Church, however, seems to suggest that when the Church exercises control to protect the institution, it is in danger of acting against the gospel of love which is its *raison d'être*: for example in the past with the Inquisitions and more recently with the covering up of sex scandals.

The Catholic Church with its highly developed set of rules and laws hopes to keep its members on the straight and narrow and eventually get them into heaven. The Church claims the authority to know precisely the mind of God down to the minutest detail and it expects Church members to obey. Some evangelical Protestant preachers also seem to know the mind of God in great detail based on a simplistic understanding of what the Bible is, while broad church Anglicanism once again lies somewhere in between. Given the fragmentation of Protestantism, largely based on individual interpretation of the Bible, one can perfectly understand why until relatively recently the Catholic Church was not in favour of putting the Bible in the hands of lay people.

The topics mentioned in the following paragraphs have been the subject of major theological controversy in the history of the Church, but I talk about them here as I believe Protestant lay people understand them.

Protestants are aware that Catholics have a different approach to the Virgin Mary from their own. The mistaken belief is widespread amongst Roman Catholics that Protestants don't believe in the Virgin Mary. However there are three feast days of the Blessed Virgin Mary in the calendar of the Church of Ireland. Protestants revere her as the mother of Jesus, despite the fact that the New Testament recounts that at the wedding feast at Cana Jesus himself was rather offhand with, if not dismissive of, his mother. To say the least he didn't speak to her in a very kindly way: 'O woman what have you to do with me?'

Protestants do not intercede through the Virgin Mary, nor indeed do they intercede through saints. Protestants go straight to the top, to God, through Jesus Christ, and see no reason they shouldn't since this is what Jesus himself in the New Testament told us to do. The idea that the God of Jesus Christ will give greater consideration to the prayers of people addressed to him through saints is not credible to Protestants. It appears that the cult of intercession through Mary and the saints gained momentum during a time in the life of the Church when the divinity of Jesus was emphasised almost to the exclusion of his humanity. This made him less accessible to ordinary sinful mortals who then developed a pantheon of saints as the most likely people to approach him on their behalf. The orthodox doctrine of the Church, however, is that Jesus was both human and divine in the one person and neither to the exclusion of the other.

There is no mechanism within Protestantism since the Reformation, certainly not within the Church of Ireland, for the creation of saints, and if there were there might not be many candidates. I find it impossible to imagine the Standing Committee of the General Synod researching nominations for sainthood, and the General Synod itself discussing the canonisation of Church of Ireland saints. The reformed traditions find it difficult to accept that God performs miracles on the intercession of saints that he would not otherwise perform. Can we really know, despite elaborate and careful procedures, that apparently miraculous healings are attributable to prayer, and to the prayer of one particularly good

Christian person who has died? Many miracles were attributed to Saint Philomena and a proper office and Mass granted to her by the Pope in the mid-nineteenth century. She was for a time one of the most popular saints on account of the devotion of a French priest, Curé d'Ars, who became the patron saint of parish priests. When subsequently the Church said she did not exist, what of the miracles it was claimed she had performed?

Can it be that God intervenes and heals people, many of whom have had fulfilled, successful and comfortable lives, as the result of fervent intercession, whether through saints for Catholics or directly for Protestants? Some religious people believe that he does and yet he allows millions of innocent little children in the Third World to suffer and die of starvation or AIDS without intervening? I can hear a reader present the argument that starvation and AIDS are the result of the sinfulness of somebody along the line and that God must allow people to have free will. Are starvation and AIDS the result of sinfulness or do they result from the vagaries of nature, and if so how does God relate to nature? Consult the theologians.

On the other hand I know a man who would attribute his recovery from alcoholism to his devotion to Padre Pio, and I respect this. Any devotion that can help an alcoholic to recovery must be respected and encouraged, but I don't know what to make of Damien Duff, or was it his mother, putting a medal of Padre Pio in his boot during the World Cup, presumably to help him to play well or even to score goals. I find this whole area extremely puzzling.

Apparitions and relics are two other difficult areas for Protestants. It has been suggested that apparitions occur in difficult economic or social times and they seem often to be the Blessed Virgin Mary appearing to children and emphasising something in particular, for example her Immaculate Conception. The Immaculate Conception is a modern doctrine of the Church, promulgated by the Pope alone in 1854 and not by a Council of the Church, which says that her conception and birth, by the special grace of God, were not tainted by sin. This popular belief among many in the Church was the subject of theological debate as far back as the Early Church. Roman Catholic lay people often confuse the doctrine of the Immaculate Conception with that of the Virgin Birth.

These apparitions seem to involve warnings to humanity of the dire consequences of sin. As far as I know the Virgin doesn't appear to Protestants. When I made this point in discussion with a Catholic priest friend recently, his response was, 'Do you blame her?' Neither do Protestants, as far as I know, have other kinds of apparitions. Some kinds of Protestants do claim to have visions to call them to repentance but this call is usually personal to themselves, doesn't carry a message to humanity at large and tends not to happen to respectable, middle-class middle-of-the-road Anglicans!

It is interesting to note that the official Catholic Church appears to have serious doubts about recent apparitions and miraculous events at Medjugorje, Ballinspittle, the House of Prayer at Achill and pictures on a wardrobe door in a flat in Ballymun. I find it hard to escape the conclusion that if Lourdes, Fatima and Knock occurred today they might not get official Church recognition either. I do not doubt that unaccountable healings take place at these shrines, but I believe they are attributable to faith as a component of the mind/body relationship, rather than to the miraculous intervention of the Blessed Virgin Mary. Then, I may be wrong. We do know much more about faith in the process of mind/body health and healing these days without needing to posit the intervention of heaven. I hold exactly the same opinion about the Ministry of Healing in Protestant Churches. This ministry helps some people to wholeness and healing and not others, and this creates a difficulty that God would discriminate between individuals in this way. Some Protestant Ministry of Healing people go so far as to make the distinction between healings that result from faith in Jesus Christ and those that don't. They espouse the former, but not the latter.

I think that Protestants find relics, and especially the attribution of miraculous powers to relics, even more difficult to understand than apparitions. Again it comes back to the fact that Catholics seem to have a greater sense of the miraculous and the supernatural than Protestants. Transubstantiation, a central doctrine of the Catholic Church, is based on the miraculous. It teaches that God miraculously transforms the substance of the elements but not their accidents. Catholic theology says that God miraculously preserved Mary in her conception and birth from the taint of original sin and miraculously assumed her bodily into heaven. It is therefore not surprising that Catholics more readily believe other miraculous events such as apparitions and moving statues. How matadors, however, can believe that prayers in a chapel beneath the bullring before a bullfight will mean that God will miraculously protect them from danger before they set out to kill a bull for entertainment is surely a bridge too far. Protestants are not immune from belief in the miraculous intervention of God in their personal affairs. I met one recently who attributed his purchase of a house and some land at well below the market price to the intervention of God as a reward for his faithfulness. Just recently a man in the United States who won the world record lotto prize worth $315 million dollars said: 'I just want to thank God for letting me pick the right numbers – or letting the machine pick the right numbers.' The newspaper report didn't say what the religion of the winner was.

Most Protestants would have no difficulty whatever acknowledging that St Teresa of Lisieux, 'The Little Flower', was a remarkable young woman who can be seen from her autobiography to have been an exceptional person. The idea, however, of touring her bones around the country in a casket is foreign to the Protestant mind. Even more foreign would be the idea that somehow contact with these bones could bestow grace or even work miracles.

Protestants understand that Catholics see such relics as tangible aids to faith. They are a reminder of a devout life worthy of imitation in its devotion to God. Catholics do not worship the bones or in the case of statues the thing itself, as some Protestants ignorant of these matters might think, but use them to focus on the life of the person represented. The danger that Protestants see is that of people substituting the relics or statues themselves for faith.

There is a danger that devotion to relics will become superstition. The Catholic chaplains of a major Dublin hospital, one I did not work in, arranged to have a certain priest removed from visiting patients because he brought around a glove, the relic of a saint, as a medium of devotion and healing. In the presence of the relics of St Teresa when they were in Ireland, people were reported to have smelled roses, the symbol of St Teresa. Even if it was only in the imagination, is it any harm? On balance perhaps the veneration of relics is good if it is simply a matter of strengthening people's faith.

A further problem Protestants have with the use of relics and statues is the danger that the person represented by them, might become a substitute in devotion for Jesus himself. The prime example of this within Catholicism is devotion to the Blessed Virgin Mary, which led at one time to a movement to have her declared co-redemptrix with Christ, which if it had been successful, would, according to Protestants, diminish the uniqueness of Christ in the scheme of salvation. Protestants use the Bible as the ultimate criterion by which to judge what to believe to ensure salvation. Whereas some areas of Catholic devotion may not have biblical warranty, if they are not required to be believed in order to ensure salvation they may be valuable aids to faith for some people.

It is possible to find in the diversity of scripture a text to support virtually any theological position or religious practice. The miraculous power of relics has been justified from biblical accounts. After his ascension into heaven Elisha took Elijah's cloak and struck the water with it, which parted, and he crossed over. A dead man, who needed to be buried in a hurry to avoid a band of marauding Moabites, was placed in Elisha's grave and as soon as he touched the bones of Elisha he came alive again and stood up. In Acts the handkerchiefs that touched Paul's body worked miraculous cures on the sick and possessed. Is it legitimate to use these texts of two thousand and more years ago to justify the use of relics today? I don't believe it is, but it probably depends on what else you believe about God and humankind.

Belief in purgatory and the use of indulgences are an insurmountable problem for most members of the reformed Churches. Protestants would believe that when a person dies the business of their soul is a matter for God and not a matter for intervention or interference from earth. The biblical authority for purgatory seems to be based on some pretty flimsy texts, for example Christ saying that the sin against the Holy Spirit is not forgiven in this world or the next, suggesting that expiation for other sins is possible after death. That anyone this side of the grave has the authority to grant indulgences to somebody on the far side of the grave is simply not credible to Protestants. That the Church sold such indulgences for money was one of the triggers of the Reformation.

Although aware that the Pope is infallible in only narrowly defined circumstances, Protestants would have difficulty accepting that any human being, even an exceptionally holy, spiritual and wise Pope is not in danger of making a mistake. Or a Pope, genuinely unaware of the fact, might have a personal prejudice or a political purpose for promulgating an infallible statement. Furthermore there seems to be a problem as to whether some of the Pope's decisions, such as his condemnation of the ordination of women, are infallible statements or not, since some Catholic theologians and Vatican officials disagree on the matter. This, however, may be a case of Protestants noting carefully and quoting reports that reinforce them in their own prejudices. Many Protestants have no difficulty in accepting that the Bishop of Rome might be the spiritual head of a united Church, but his role would have to be carefully defined.

The Second Vatican Council was a watershed in the life of the Roman Catholic Church in modern times. It appears to outsiders that there are two opinions within Catholicism about the changes that it brought about. A conservative opinion seems to be that many of the present ills of the Church are attributable to some of the liberalising changes of the Second Vatican Council and the Church must row back on these. The progressive/liberal opinion is that the current state of the Church results from the evolution of society at large and the best hope for the Church at a difficult time is to hold her nerve and implement fully the reforms of the Second Vatican Council.

Many Protestants view the difficulties of the Catholic Church in Ireland today with the same sadness, as do many Roman Catholics. Here I am not only referring to clerical child sex abuse by a tiny minority of priests, or the abuse of children in orphanages and women in Magdalene Laundries by some religious. I refer to the general diminution in religious belief and practice. The contrast in Catholicism between the Ireland I grew up in the 1940s and 1950s and that of today is enormous.

Right up to the Second Vatican Council in the early 1960s Catholics were not allowed to attend services in Protestant churches, let alone receive communion. After the Council the practice grew up slowly that at services marking significant events, especially weddings, Catholics would receive communion in Protestant churches. When President Mary McAleese, a Catholic, received communion in the St Patrick's Church of Ireland Cathedral it brought the matter to a head. Cardinal Connell, Archbishop of Dublin, seemed to say that Church of Ireland communion was 'a sham' for which comment he later apologised. The Catholic bishops of England, Ireland, Scotland and Wales issued a document forbidding Catholics to receive communion in a Protestant church and forbidding Catholic priests from giving communion to Protestants. However Catholics, perhaps not in as great numbers, still receive Communion in Protestant Churches.

Cardinal Connell appealed to Church of Ireland clergy not to invite Roman Catholics to receive communion. He seemed to imply that Church of Ireland clergy were encouraging Catholics to break the rules of their Church. This was not the case. It was simply a matter of clergy putting members of other religions, including members of other Protestant denominations, at their ease and saying that as far as the Church of Ireland was concerned they were welcome to receive communion should they wish to. Why did he appeal in this way to clergy of another denomination?

The cardinal's approach was in stark contrast to the way in which Archbishop McQuaid, when he ruled the roost over thirty years earlier, would have dealt with the issue. He would simply have issued an instruction for Catholics not to receive communion in the churches of other denominations and that would have been the end of the matter.

Protestants have been on the sideline observing all these changes and while the majority have sympathy with their Catholic friends and neighbours in the Church's difficulties, it has to be said there are undoubtedly some Protestants bigots who would say: 'I told you so.'

Whereas the Second Vatican Council did not alter any essential doctrine of the Church, it did alter things in the area of Church practice and order. For example the change from Latin to the vernacular in the liturgy. This led to the same reaction as occurred in the Church of Ireland to the change from Tudor English to contemporary English in the liturgy – some readily accepted the change and some resisted it. How can it be a sin pre-Second Vatican Council to go to the funeral of a neighbour in a Protestant church, when post-Second Vatican Council there are often more Catholics than Protestants at Protestant funerals in rural Ireland and it is not a sin? Protestants believe that a sin is a sin and will always be a sin. An uninformed Protestant might say, without wishing to be irreverent, that somebody changed their mind and it was hardly God himself but somebody acting on his behalf. Is it fair that somebody might have ended up in purgatory or hell in the old days for sins that are no longer sins today? I know that this is a very Protestant way of looking at things, and I'm sure it is not as simple as it sounds.

In a similar vein Protestants would have difficulties with the fact that limbo, formerly the destination of babies who died unbaptised, now no longer exists. How does a mother who in the past was told her unbaptised baby was in limbo feel now that it has been abolished. I have a feeling that in discussing this kind of thing we might have to consult some theologian who hasn't yet got a proper job. If you think I'm a bit prejudiced against theologians I am not the only one: another writer recounts, 'Erasmus was always ready to show contempt for the pompous obscurity of professional theologians!'

What I have said above is, I believe, a fair account of the average Protestant perspective on some aspects of Roman Catholicism. Most of the critical issues are highly theological and I know that for the theologically informed I have not done them justice. I am happy to leave them to our friends the theologians who are expert in dealing in the kinds of abstractions that the average Church member of any persuasion does not understand. I simply want to recount some Roman Catholic theological issues as I believe the average lay member of one of the reformed traditions would see them.

However it is striking that in all the doctrinal issues that occupy all the Churches when discussing matters that are central to their concern, there is almost never mention of one commodity. That is love, Christian love, *agape*, the commodity in which Jesus himself summed up his teaching, and which the average Church member understands more readily than doctrine. When a lawyer put Jesus on the spot and asked him what was the greatest commandment of all, he didn't launch into an exposition on the necessity of belief in abstract theological doctrines. He didn't give an exposition on his relationship to God the Father and the Holy Spirit. He didn't take the opportunity to say how he was both God and man, and he certainly didn't give any hint that people who disagreed on these kinds of issue should maim, mutilate, torture or burn each other. He summarised his teaching of love your enemy, do good to those who despitefully use you, turn the other cheek, forgive seventy times seven, judge not that you be not judged. He said: 'You shall love the Lord your God with all your heart, and with all your soul and with all your mind. This is the first and great commandment and the second is like it, you shall love your neighbour as yourself. On these two commandments depend all the law and the prophets.' Why has the history of the Christian Church not been primarily a working out of Christ's own summary of his teaching of love? Could it possibly have something to do with Lord Acton?

13

The Church

'An' many a head was broken, aye, an' many an eye was shut,
Whin practisin' manoeuvres with Slattery's Mounted Fut.'
Percy French 'Slattery's Mounted Fut'

Every time I hear this song it reminds me of the violence of the conflict between different factions at some of the early Church Councils. A conflict, let's not forget, over opposing theological positions on the nature of the Prince of Peace. The victors, who defined orthodox Christian doctrine, then paraded through the streets with their supporters shouting campaign slogans. The early Councils were convened by the Roman emperors whose main concerns were to achieve unanimity, which they promoted by the threat to banish dissenters to the remotest parts of the empire. Proceedings became so violent at one Council that the emperor had to send in the troops to clear delegates from the hall. These Councils were a little livelier than your average synod of bishops in Rome or session of the Church of Ireland General Synod, but almost certainly not less political.

After Jesus' ascension the disciples dispersed abroad to preach the gospel of the good news of love and forgiveness. People began to reflect on questions such as the relationship between God the Father and Jesus and how the Holy Spirit fitted into the scheme of things. Needless to say there were no quick and easy answers and different people took different positions on these matters and felt strongly about them. Councils were held and agreement arrived at with the guidance of the Holy Spirit and the help of some of the persuasive methods mentioned above. Those who opposed were discredited, banished and declared heretics.

During the first thousand years of the Church emperors called Councils of the Church to adjudicate on what was orthodox Christian teaching and what was not. Over the years a body of doctrine emanated from Councils of the Church and became official Church teaching. In the second millennium it was Popes who called Councils of the Church to regulate the doctrine or discipline of the Church.

In the first two General Councils in the fourth century for example the central doctrine of the Christian Church, the doctrine of the Trinity, was laid down. It says that God exists in three persons and one substance. This sounds simple enough until you begin to think about it and analyse what it means. If you do this you cannot by definition arrive at a conclusion, because as one textbook puts it:

> The doctrine of the Trinity is held to be a mystery in the strict sense, in that it can neither be known by unaided human reason apart from revelation, nor cogently demonstrated by reason after it has been revealed.

In other words it is not possible to understand it, and when the Church comes to the point that it requires its members to believe something that it is not possible to understand they call it a mystery, and until the seventeenth century, or even later, you were in danger of being burned to death if you did not believe it. In many cases before they burned you they tortured you to try to get you to recant. If you held firm to your views they tied your hands behind your back and tied you to a stake and lit a fire at your feet so that you burned slowly from the feet up. If, however, you had held heretical views on a previous occasion and had recanted of them then, on this occasion, they might, as a concession, hit you on the head and knock you out first. Or they might strangle you if you didn't express your genuinely held heresy too adamantly. Burning with or without the concession of being knocked out or strangled first was your fate for having the temerity to disagree with the Church.

Over the years the Christian Church committed this and many other kinds of appalling atrocity against people who chose to dissent from orthodox doctrine. Torture was used with official Church approval. They cut out people's tongues and they gouged out people's eyes. In the early twelfth century they gouged out the eyes of a large group of heretics in the south of France, the Cathars or Albigensians. They gouged out only one eye of one man so that he could see where he was going and walk at the front while others walked behind with hands on the shoulder of the one in front. How kind of the people who did this evil thing to make this concession to one man, but of course this wasn't kindness or a concession. They left the leader with one eye so that he could lead the column of the blind to the next village to warn them what the fate of heretics there would be if they continued to defy the Church. These persecutors were acting in the name of the God of love who was in Jesus Christ. Jesus who taught his followers to love each other, to forgive seventy times seven, to turn the other cheek, to love their enemies.

If there is a final judgement can you imagine the Popes and the leaders of other Churches that authorised these kinds of atrocities, saying when confronted by God, 'But Lord, they defied the truth so we had to punish them, they were unsound theologically on the doctrine of the Trinity.'

'And what about my teaching of love and forgiveness?'

'Oh, we never thought of that.'

When Jesus told the parable of the Good Samaritan, I wonder why he didn't have the Samaritan say to the man who had been beaten up something like the following: 'Now before I give this innkeeper money to look after you I want you to assure me that you believe that the Holy Ghost was Jesus' father. I want you to tell me you believe that Jesus is of one substance with his Father, not of like substance but of the same substance. If you don't tell me that you firmly believe this, not only can I not help you, but I'll have to kill you instead.'

During the Reformation period the Anglican Church, through the authority of Queen Elizabeth I, executed Roman Catholics for their dissent. Calvinists burned people as heretics, most notably Servetus, a native of Navarre, who escaped the Inquisition in

France and through Calvin's good offices was burned in Geneva for his denial of the Doctrine of the Trinity. The Church over the centuries persecuted and executed Jews and made them wear a yellow mark in public, something the Nazis adopted in our own time. Persecution of the Jews was not the prerogative of Catholics. One historian refers to a passage from Luther in 1543 as a blueprint for the Nazis' Kristallnacht of 1938.

The Church and subsequently Protestants throughout Europe between the fifteenth and eighteenth centuries burned and hanged women as witches. (You will be glad to know that only two women were done to death as witches in Ireland). The Bible does in fact prescribe the death penalty for witches. (Exodus 22 v 18). These atrocities spread to America where the infamous execution of nineteen witches at Salem, Massachusetts, took place. These unfortunate women, and some men too, were part of a vast collective fantasy indulged in by their inquisitors, and many of the victims were easily persuaded that the things they were accused of doing actually happened, when in fact they did not. Christians of all kinds killed each other; one group was as bad as the other. In the light of the teachings of Jesus Christ they were all guilty of the most appalling atrocities. For the life of me I cannot understand why they did not see that what they were doing was evil and a travesty of the Gospel they claimed to promote.

People trivialise this behaviour with the lame excuse, 'Oh, they were different times'. They certainly were different times when the life of the Church was primarily a tyranny of the constant threat of excommunication and damnation, rather than a eucharistic fellowship of love and forgiveness. The threat of punishment dominated rather than hope and promise of eternal peace. People will say we live in softer times: these were hard men. They certainly were hard men. If women had been in charge it might have been different, or it might not. These men were self-opinionated prelates and pastors who suffered from the delusion that they had unique access to absolute truth.

Here is where Lord Acton comes in. Much of what they did had nothing whatever to do with the Gospel, it was to do with power and control. Lord Acton's famous dictum, 'power tends to corrupt, and absolute power corrupts absolutely', applies to the Church and enlightens us on this matter. If you read the gospels the one thing Jesus did not seem to be interested in was power. In fact he preached love which requires vulnerability, the very opposite of power. He wandered around Palestine and as he bumped into people, or as they came to him, he loved them while well aware of their humanity and their sin, he healed them and he taught them forgiveness. The writer of St Matthew's gospel tells us he had a tough streak too; he said: 'Do not think I have come to bring peace on earth ... but a sword.' A look at the history of the Church shows that he wasn't wrong about that.

Jesus knocked around with ordinary people, mainly fishermen. In his band he even had a civil servant from the equivalent of the Revenue Commissioners and a zealot, perhaps the equivalent of a member of Sinn Féin. There is no evidence that Jesus himself was bothered by the Roman occupation of Palestine. He willingly healed the Roman centurion's daughter and as an officer of an occupying army he showed no evidence of wanting to assassinate him. Jesus wouldn't have thought much of some of the people at our recent tribunals since he said, 'Render to Caesar the things that are Caesar's ...' In modern parlance 'give up your auld sins' and pay your income tax. Jesus consorted with the marginalised, with social outcasts. His favourite targets were the leaders of the religious establishment, and his favourite word for them was 'hypocrites.' I wonder what his favourite word would be for the leaders of today's religious establishments. The idea that he intended to found the Church that developed through history as a power-crazy, doctrine-obsessed and largely love-starved organisation, is simply not credible.

The General Councils of the Church must surely reflect the life and concerns of the Church fairly accurately. Reading a history of the Generals Councils recently I could not find the use of the word 'love' once. Maybe Patrick Kavanagh in his poem 'Lough Derg' throws some light on the matter:

Christ was lately dead,
Men were afraid
With a new fear, the fear
Of love.

The Councils of the Church were concerned either with weighty doctrinal definitions or Church order and reform. To read the history of the Church from this perspective you would think that love had nothing to do with the Church, whereas it seems to me that love is what Christianity is all about. Violence in society was a concern of one of the mediaeval Councils, and one of the canons issued at the end of that Council decreed that fighting could only take place on Mondays, Tuesdays and Wednesdays throughout the year, but not at all during the Advent-Christmas-Epiphany and Lent-Easter-Pentecost seasons!

If you are in any doubt that power and not love was the motivating force of the Church, especially in the Middle Ages, how about the famous contest between Pope Gregory VII and Henry IV the Holy Roman Emperor. Over the years since Constantine, emperors and Popes have had uneasy relationships with each other, to put it mildly. Each wanted to be top dog. Popes took the line that when Jesus had gone back to heaven he had appointed them as his representative on earth, therefore Popes and not emperors were rulers of the world. Furthermore at different points in the history of the Church they bolstered this claim with the use of forged documents.

Gregory, who was trying admirably to reform the life of the Church (for example he forbade the burning of witches) was displeased that Henry was interfering in the Church's affairs. Gregory proscribed lay investiture, that is the need for approval of Church appointments by the secular authorities, as part of his reforms in 1075 AD and as you can imagine emperors and kings around Europe weren't too pleased by this development. When Gregory threatened to depose him if he didn't knuckle under, Henry called synods and declared the Pope deposed. Gregory in turn excommunicated Henry and relieved Henry's subjects of their oath of allegiance to him and threatened anyone who supported or served him with excommunication. In fear of the damnation of their immortal souls princes and subjects began to withdraw their support from Henry and his position became desperate.

Henry went to Italy to try to have his excommunication and deposition lifted, where he found the Pope staying at the castle at Canossa. The Pope humiliated him and made him stand in the snow in his underpants fasting for four days and praying to God that the Pope would relent. Having done his penance the Pope reinstated Henry who soon got into Church/State machinations again and Gregory excommunicated him again. This time, no doubt with Canossa still fresh in his memory, Henry appointed an anti-Pope and marched on Rome. After a two-year siege Gregory fled and died at Salerno without returning to Rome. This entire saga was conducted in the pursuit of power, not of love.

There were of course exceptions in the life of the Church throughout history. There was a minority of people in the mystical tradition, many of whom did not escape brushes of one kind or another with Church authority. Hildegard of Bingen was a twelfth century German mystic. Her convent was for a time placed under a Church interdict because somebody who had died excommunicate was buried near her church. Meister Eckhart, a fourteenth century Dominican mystic and a controversial figure was tried for heresy but died before the Pope made a decision on his case. There was St Teresa of Avila, a sixteenth century Spanish Carmelite nun and mystic and St John of the Cross, of the dark nights of the soul, who co-operated with St Teresa in founding the Order of Discalced Carmelites, and there were many others. There were people too who, in the name of Jesus, had a great deal of love for their fellow human beings. The name that comes to mind immediately is Francis of Assisi, who for a time was not the Pope's favourite person, but who, wait for it, voluntarily gave up control of his Order because he realised he hadn't got the qualities for supervising or administering it. He was more concerned for his work with the poor than the exercise of power and control. Apart altogether from his life's work, voluntarily giving up control is in itself enough to make him a saint.

For some reason it seems to be a short step from wanting to save souls to wanting power over people. I don't know why this is the case but it appears to be so. Perhaps it is the belief that if people are allowed to hold different beliefs they make us feel insecure about our own and it follows that if we can prove that our beliefs come directly from God then the beliefs of others must be false. They are therefore inferior and we can, usually by threats and by fear, force them to comply and label them 'heretics' if they do not. Today we don't use the term 'heretic' often, preferring terms like 'separated brethren'. There was a heresy trial in the Church of Ireland recently, but it was abandoned after one session; it should never have been started in the first place.

Isn't it a marvellous thing that today Christians are not burning or hanging people who disagree with them. The question is: how the devil, if you'll excuse the expression, did it take Christians the best part of two thousand years to begin, and it is still only a beginning, to respect each other's right to hold different opinions on religious questions?

I see two main themes in the life and teaching of Jesus Christ as recounted in the gospels – love and salvation. They seem to me to be interrelated; I believe salvation is achieved through a life of love and forgiveness. As we reflect on the world and the place of human beings in it we are confronted with a mystery. We have no answers to the myriad of questions it occurs to us to ask. The Christian Church claims that Jesus Christ is the answer. He Himself is recorded as having said 'I am the way, the truth and the life.' I believe that life for human beings has meaning and purpose when they live lives of love as we see love in the life and teaching of Jesus.

This is not a 'motherhood and apple pie' kind of love. It is unconditional, self-giving and often costly love. It means accepting that other people have as much right to hold views that differ from us, as we have to hold ours. It means forgiving people who wrong us, as we would want to be forgiven when we wrong others. This kind of love is the only hope for people of whatever religion. This kind of love is not exclusive to Christianity and it is not uncommon for people who claim no religion to practise it as well or

better than many Christians. This love is salvation for humankind.
When the rich young ruler asked Jesus what he must do to be
saved, Jesus enumerated the commandments, which he summarised elsewhere as, 'love God and love your neighbour as yourself'.
He answered the salvation question with the love answer. In other
words he said that love was the means of salvation.

I see no evidence from the gospels that Jesus required adher-
ence to abstract theological doctrines, composed by theological
geniuses and which the average Church member cannot understand, to be enforced by fear and the threat of eternal damnation.
Where salvation is getting to heaven after death, rather than living
a life of love in this life the Church used fear of excommunication
and hell as instruments to exercise power and control over people.
Christian loving was a minority activity at a time when judgement
and condemnation of others, considered doctrinally defective, were
the order of the day. It appears that where there was theological
certainty, and salvation was based on fear, then there was abuse of
power and Christian love went out the window.

What is the situation today? Most Christians of different traditions are beginning to get sense. They have learned that while dis-
agreeing on some aspects of doctrine they can respect each other and
attend each other's services, but for the Roman Catholic Church this
does not yet include receiving communion in each other's church. It
is hoped that in due course this will come. On civic occasions wor-
shipping together even extends to Jews and Muslims.

Today most people of different religions want to work together at a practical level in a way that wasn't possible in the past
when the Churches were obsessed with doctrinal matters. Today
it is quite usual to find mutual co-operation between members of
the different Christian Churches working at the task of being the
Church in the world. The love and care and support I received
from the Catholic chaplains when I arrived at the different hospitals and prisons, as a complete greenhorn to chaplaincy, was truly
enriching for me. In the hospitals the Catholic chaplains on duty
would keep an eye on Church of Ireland patients I was anxious
about at weekends, since I couldn't be in the hospital on Saturdays

and Sundays. One sister chaplain once said to me: 'I say the Lord's Prayer with any of your patients I visit because I know you use the Lord's prayer too.' I much appreciated her sensitivity. Many Church of Ireland patients expressed to me their appreciation of visits from Catholic chaplains, and I in turn visited Catholic patients from time to time. This kind of thing in some places is now quite the norm. That there are still doctrinal differences between the Churches is irrelevant to the loving care and co-operation between their ministries.

The same is true at parish level, and has been for many years. One parish priest who was not allowed by the rules of his Church to conduct a service of blessing for a parishioner who was marrying a divorcee, asked his opposite number, the Church of Ireland rector, if he could do anything for them. The rector provided a service of blessing on their civil marriage in his church. The parish priest and his curate attended and took part, along with the choir and some parishioners from the Catholic parish and some Church of Ireland parishioners. They had the most marvellous service of celebration of the commitment of two people to each other, one of whom had failed on a previous occasion and had no doubt been forgiven by God. It was of course a service of blessing and not a marriage. This enriching celebration observed the spirit of the law, if not the letter, and as we know 'the letter kills and the spirit gives life'. You may be dying of curiosity to know where this service was held, but I'm not telling you!

These manifestations of love between Christians are slowly taking the place of the theological and doctrinal stand-offs of the past. There is of course a place for theology, though I'm not sure the average citizen agrees. Leave doctrine, that in the past was the cause of so much hatred and bitterness, to the theologians to sort out. It is an excellent thing that in the meantime ordinary Church members, clergy and religious are working together with love to serve this mysterious world.

I have no doubt in my mind that if Jesus arrived back on a village street in Ireland today, not the second coming, but simply in the flesh like the first time, everybody would want to claim him as their own. Can't you imagine Catholics pressing forward in the crowd saying, 'Haven't we got it right about transubstantiation? Isn't it true that your mother was conceived and born immaculately?' The Protestants would be shouting at him: 'Aren't we right about justification by faith alone? Isn't it right that the Bible is your infallible word, and the only rule of faith? This way to the parochial house. This way to the rectory.' I can see the sadness in his eyes and the quiet dignity as he, ignoring the questions, makes his way slowly through the crowd not to the parish priest or the rector but to search out the lonely, the marginalised and the unloved.

If he arrived in Dublin I doubt if he would go near either of the archbishops or other Church leaders. Indeed he might have harsh words to say to them as he did to the religious establishment first time round. Can you imagine the raised eyebrows in Drumcondra and Temple Road if he took the No. 11 bus to Clonskeagh to see the Imam there. I believe he would be far more likely to go to the prisons and hospitals and to find out Father Peter McVerry and his work with boys in trouble, Sister Stan and her work for the homeless, the employment scheme of the Presbyterians in Parnell Square, the social outreach projects of all the other Churches and especially the work of St Vincent de Paul and the Salvation Army. He would, I have no doubt, find out and approve projects for the development of people in deprived areas, like the Shanty Project in Tallaght, which have no explicit religious connection other than sheer love and care for people. The criterion of Christian authenticity is love and not doctrine. Love unites people across all kinds of human barriers while doctrine divides. No doubt there would be someone who would want to ask Jesus some theological conundrums. For example the one that occupied some people at the time of the world's first heart transplant, as to whether it was all right to transplant a Catholic heart into a Protestant or a Protestant heart into a Catholic!

14

Believe It or Not

There are two aspects to the life of the Church: the vertical and the horizontal, as it were. The vertical has to do with belief in God – doctrine, worship and such matters as life after death. The horizontal has to do with the here and now, the world in which we live, how we treat each other and how Church members ought to conduct themselves in this world.

I believe that there is no problem in this world that love cannot solve. By that I mean Christian love, *agape*, self-giving love that is often costly for the giver. This kind of love accepts that you don't have to wait for someone to be perfect or even to agree with you before you love them. This is not romantic, erotic or sentimental love. It is the love that Jesus Christ showed to those he met in his time on earth. If Hitler, Stalin, Idi Amin, Pol Pot, rather than becoming intoxicated with, and corrupted by, power, had this love as their guiding principle for governing their people how different things would have been. Can you even begin to get your mind around the quantity of evil that those four dictators perpetrated against humankind, let alone all the other evil rulers and dictators throughout history who were driven by the lust for power.

After the unfathomable amount of evil perpetrated by these, and many other, tyrants, everything they set out to achieve eventually came to nothing, absolutely nothing. All they achieved was human death and suffering on an unimaginable scale. While the Church of Jesus Christ, not the infallible Church, but the broken Church comprising fallible sinful human beings, despite all it divisions and faults, and despite its own obsession with control, has made some positive contribution to humankind. Not as much as some might like to think, but where the Church does contribute to the world it does so from the love of her members and not from her obsession with doctrine. The Church, of course, has also caused death and suffering when the guiding principles have been other than love.

People from the other world religions – Islam, Hinduism, Buddhism and others – and some atheists and agnostics also make a major contribution to humankind. They do immense good, and where they do so they do it from the same kind of motivation as Christians, namely, love for their fellow human beings. On one occasion Hilary and I walked up a dirt track, like the dried-up bed of a mountain stream, in a line of people to a Sufi shrine in the hills outside Islamabad in Pakistan. On the other side of the track there were people coming down. We were the only white faces there. Twice in the course of the ascent men crossed the path to shake my hand. The first simply said, 'Welcome' and twenty minutes later another came over to me, shook my hand and said one word only: 'Brother'. Their Islamic beliefs would not allow them greet Hilary, a woman. They wanted to express their love, and if you have difficulty calling these spontaneous gestures love, then that's your problem, not mine.

Years of sanctions caused the death and suffering of thousands and thousands of Iraqis, mainly children. Would there have been a war if, instead of sanctions, America and Europe had flooded Iraq with medical and economic aid? Naive you may say. I'm not so sure. Can you imagine how things might have been if George Bush and Saddam Hussein were so motivated by love and justice for people that they were prepared to do anything to serve them rather than indulge their addiction to power? It sounds ridiculous but think about it. If you do think all of this is naive, then Jesus was naïve. The misuse of power is the enemy of love.

It's not so ridiculous when you consider that love *en masse* is justice, and I use the word justice here to mean fairness for all, a just society. It is impossible for a person to love more than a relatively small number of people, so to love large numbers of people you ensure they have justice. Justice in the sense that people have human dignity in their daily lives, a justice that acknowledges the intrinsic human worth of every individual. George Bush's responsibility is justice for the betterment of the rural poor of the Appalachians or for America's urban poor, rather than his pursuit of oil or to indulge his addiction to power by bombing Iraqis. Saddam Hussein's responsibility was to provide medical help for Iraqi children rather than indulge his addiction to power by building palaces and torturing and executing anyone who disagreed with him. If justice had been the concern of both they could have, to paraphrase Isaiah, turned their battleships into cargo vessels, and their tanks into combine harvesters. They could apply their war budgets to the advancement of their people and put many of the world's arms manufacturers out of business, and maybe collapse the world's economy in the process. In due course, however, the greed of the world's arms manufacturers would devise ways of building a commercial empire on something else. You don't have to study theology to know that love and justice are preferable to torturing, gassing and bombing the hell out of people, and they are inimical to the corruption of power.

I recently asked a clergyman friend approaching retirement after over forty-five years in the ministry, 'What's the Gospel really about?' He replied, 'It's about loving the hell out of people.' Try applying the principle that love can solve all human problems, to any human situation you know, personal, family, national or international, and see if it is true. I believe it is. I can hear some people saying: 'He's off his head, this is all romantic idealism, he's not taking account of the doctrine of original sin.'

I'm as aware of original sin as anyone. In fact it is the only Christian doctrine I have no difficulty with, in that it describes credibly our human nature. Not, however, that there was an antecedent state of unalloyed happiness. I can verify it by looking into my own heart and by observing how people behave in the world around me. 'Man is very far-gone from original righteousness, and is of his own nature inclined to evil', as one of the Anglican articles of religion says, but I obviously don't believe 'a fall' happened. I believe that our so-called 'fallen' nature developed as an integral part of the evolution of the species from the beginning, and had to do with our struggle for survival. The story of the Garden of Eden was devised to account for human nature and to lay the blame for it on human beings rather than on the creator, God.

Christianity has endured and, I believe in some shape or form, it will endure because at its core there is this truth about the human condition, its so-called fallenness – original sin, to which it offers an answer in the person and work of Jesus Christ. This in turn offers a solution to the great human fear, death – the grim reaper, the leveller that even emperors and kings must account to. As Shirley says in 'Death the Leveller':

> The glories of our blood and state,
> Are shadows not substantial things;
> There is no armour against fate;
> Death lays his icy hand on kings:
> Sceptre and crown
> Must tumble down,
> And in the dust be equal made
> With the poor crooked scythe and spade.

If this poem had been written three or four thousand years before it was, and if some emperors in China and Egypt had read it and taken it to heart, they might have saved themselves a great deal of trouble. If this had happened, however, we wouldn't have some of the great archaeological treasures of the world. The terracotta warriors of China, designed to ensure the safe transition of the emperor Qin to the next world, would not be there and the contents of the tomb of Tutankhamen, intended to establish his kingly status in the next life would not exist. I have a feeling neither of these fine gentlemen got any further than their tombs, but of course I might be wrong.

I never did get an answer to the question of what was the potential immortal status of people of so-called pagan cultures that died before Christ came. At one time I believe the Church said they went to limbo to await the final judgement. I asked this question of one particular holy and religious Protestant woman who had no doubts about anything, and she didn't think much of their chances. She did however go on to affirm in no uncertain terms that there couldn't be anyone alive today that hadn't had the opportunity of hearing the gospel message. Even in the remotest parts of the world there was nowhere that Christian missionaries had not reached, and anyone who accepted the message would go to heaven and anyone who didn't would go to hell. Simple as that, and as she accepted the message, lock, stock and barrel she knew precisely where she was going.

There is another reason why I believe the Christian faith will endure. There is a deep desire in human beings for ritual to express their human dependence on something outside themselves and their attempts to apprehend the mystery of life. This need for ritual says: 'I don't really know what it's all about, but what Jesus did and said in his life and left us in the Eucharist expresses admirably that mystery for me.' Other world religions have their own distinctive ways of doing this. My own complete ignorance of these other religions was impressed on me recently when in Xian, the ancient capital of China, I stood in a Buddhist temple as people lit sticks of incense. Without any effort on my part to induce it, I had the most wonderful feeling of peace and contentment with myself and the world. This came about, I believe, from the atmosphere of the temple, the ritual of the incense and the incense itself; all unlikely for a lapsed Irish Protestant! There is a great danger that the adherents of any religion may be arrogant about the exclusiveness of their own rituals and worship.

Saying why one does not believe in the Christian faith is much the same as saying why one does. To put it simply, one either believes or one doesn't. I moved from believing to not believing over a number of years. I found it no longer credible that there was a creator God who intervenes in the world. This was for a combination of reasons, amongst them the incompatibility of suffering and the existence of an all-powerful and all-loving God. This is the old theodicy problem that has never been satisfactorily countered. Difficulties also arose for me from the insights of critical study of the Bible, the theory of evolution and the nature of the universe.

Some people have an admirably simple faith that sustains them through life and others by their very nature are sceptics. Jesus is reported to have said that unless we become as little children we cannot enter the Kingdom of Heaven and yet there was Thomas, the doubter. The writer of the fourth gospel, however, was careful to let us know that Thomas believed in the end. Many of the great saints of the Church acknowledged difficulties with belief. John of the Cross had his dark nights of the soul, and Julian of Norwich, who must have been a racing woman, talked about the 'flinty furlongs'. She also, by the way, believed that the clue to all problems of existence lay in Divine Love. Even Jesus himself doubted, in fact despaired. The writers of St Mark's and St Matthew's gospels record Jesus, quoting one of the Psalms, crying in anguish as he hung on the cross: 'My God, My God, why hast thou forsaken me?' If that's not doubt I don't know what is.

There are different degrees of believing. There are, of course, people who have a strong genuine belief that allows of little, if any, doubt. However, I believe that amongst regular churchgoers there are many who don't believe for themselves in that kind of way, but simply accept the teachings of the Church on trust from the clergy, whom they think know and believe it all. Those foolish people, for many clergy of all denominations have many more doubts and questions than they are prepared to admit to. In an intensely religious culture like Ireland it doesn't do for people, especially the clergy, to voice their doubts. Then there are people, like myself, who no longer believe and are in danger of being considered pariahs.

At a party recently I met a well-known, highly intelligent, successful, churchgoing Protestant retired businessman, who both invests on the stock market and goes racing and is a pillar of his Church. He informed me perfectly seriously that he didn't believe in evolution. There were too many gaps he said. The problem of the missing link. I was so flabbergasted I forgot to ask him if he thought the earth was flat. There are many theologians in the United States, particularly in the southern States, who have been funded by wealthy interests to come up with some proof that the world was created according to the early chapters of Genesis.

There are some brilliant scientific minds that are also brilliant theologically, who try to reconcile science and Christianity; the name Polkinghorne comes to mind. I have never read him because

I heard of him after I decided to do my own theology. Now I am going to give you my average punter's take on the matter. If you think I might disturb your faith perhaps you had better put down this book now and go and do something useful like dusting around the ornaments on the mantelpiece or putting those photographs from last year's holiday into the family album.

I have very little scientific knowledge since I was ejected from the science class at school after the Bunsen burner and put into the commerce class, a subject I found slightly less puzzling, and more congenial because the commerce master used to end the class with a sports quiz. From what I read, Stephen Hawking has said that time and space began with a big bang about 15 billion years ago. I also read in a newspaper (*The Irish Times*), that in *A Brief History of Time*, which I tried to read and couldn't, Hawking says that developing theories of the universe have 'profound implications for the role of God as creator.' If what he says about the big bang 15 billion years ago is true, then it certainly raises some questions for the traditional Christian view of a creator God.

The Irish Times science guru, William Reville says, apart from his prayers, that 'the earth was formed about 4.6 billion years ago. Sedimentary rocks were forming 3.8 billion years ago and traces of life are discernible in these rocks from 3.5 billion years ago.' Now you may be sceptical about the conclusions I come to in due course since the source of my scientific knowledge is newspapers, and conventional wisdom says you shouldn't believe everything you read in newspapers. Naturally I'm a sceptic about conventional wisdom too. The problem with reading books about science is the same as reading theological books. Even if you could understand them there's always another book to contradict the one you've just read and if you went on like that the time would come to die before you had time to make up your own mind about anything.

Another source of my scientific knowledge is a friend who comes in for a chat in the evenings from time to time. He is a retired university physics lecturer, and he tells me that there are more galaxies in the universe than there are grains of sand on all the beaches and deserts in the world. That the distance across our galaxy, the Milky Way, is 100 million light years, and light travels at 186,000 miles per second. What would Peter Kelly at his farm-yard gate have thought of that? He also tells me that a protozoa or amoeba crawled out of the sea onto a beach millions of years ago, and from this minute form of life we human beings evolved. It's hard to blame my retired businessman for his difficulties with evolution, but the alternative, some kind of creationism, is even more incredible. I find I have no option but to accept all of these things the scientists say, despite some niggling unease that these guys always seem to quote neat round figures ending in lots of zeros!

I accept all these facts and I have tried to reconcile them with traditional Christian theology, as I understand it. But since I haven't time to read Polkinghorne, *et al*, I end up having to accept that if there is a creator God, which I don't believe there is, having caused the big bang, he sat around for billions of years waiting for the universe to evolve. He seems, however, to have created much more than he needed when you consider the unfathomable immensity of the universe according to my retired physics lecturer friend. Even within our own solar system, which is only a minute fraction of one grain of sand, it appears that there is human life only on earth, and whether there is any kind of life anywhere else in the immensity of the universe we do not know. God must then have sat waiting until the protozoa crawled out of the sea and waited some more millions of years until animal life evolved into humans and arrived at the stage that it had a soul. In due course because humans were not behaving themselves he sent to earth prophets first and then he eventually sent Jesus, who according to the Doctrine of the Trinity was not created but was part of the Godhead and so was in on the whole business from the beginning. For me, as Professor Vokes in the Divinity School in Trinity used to say, 'this is a real problem'.

Recently a letter writer to *The Irish Times* on the same kind of theme did not seem to have any problem on this score. I quote:

> The creator has infinite patience. Having set the seeds of evolution in progress he can wait for his plan to unfold, perhaps with a nudge now and then. Mammals had to evolve to a certain stage before he could

communicate his plan to them through the prophets. And free-will had to lead us astray before he intervened by sending a Messiah.

I am prepared to accept the scientific theory that may not be credible to most religious people. That as the universe expanded after the big bang, one planet, earth, in one tiny solar system in one of the millions of galaxies that there are, happened by chance to have the critical balance of physical conditions to allow life as we know it to evolve. When the animals at the top of the evolutionary process had evolved to the point that they could ask questions about themselves, and realised how dependent for survival they were on factors outside their control, they constructed a god to appease in order to enhance their chances of survival. For some this god was the sun, without which survival was not possible, and different people around the earth focused on different gods, some of which they physically made themselves.

In addition to their problems about their physical survival on earth, when they developed the capacity, they began to reflect on their origin and destiny – where they came from and where they were going. As they evolved, they developed a moral sense by which they created criteria which said something like this. God created us, if you behave in a certain kind of way, pray to him, appease him and even offer sacrifices to him, he will make sure you have enough to eat and when you die you will survive into the next world. Now the gurus who came up with this kind of thing soon realised that most people were afraid of starvation and of death. This way they could get the people, from fear of these fates, to behave as they wanted them to behave; they started to exercise power and control over them. This power was sweet so they took control of the rituals and beliefs in order to copper fasten their control of the people, and part of this was to say which individuals would survive into the next world and which would not. Does all this ring a bell?

In the scale of things, relatively recently, a few thousand years ago, one particular tribe of people in the Middle East, the Jews, decided that, not only was there only one God, but that they, the

Jews, were his chosen people. They believed that God would look after them if they were faithful to him, and he would help them to overcome their enemies. It doesn't ring true to me, however, that a universal God would have favourites, and if he had it was unfair of him. For example, if you and I had been residents of Jericho we would have been a bit miffed that God had given us into the hands of the Israelites. It was hardly fair that God gave the Jews a way of knocking down the walls so that they 'utterly destroyed all in the city, both men and women, young and old, sheep and asses, with the edge of the sword.' Not only was God involved but if, according to the doctrine of the Trinity, Jesus was part of the Godhead from the beginning then he was implicated in this atrocity. If such an atrocity took place in war today it would be contrary to the Geneva Convention.

The next stage of the process is even more difficult. Don't you think that if God wanted to come on earth in the form of a man that it would only have been fair for him to give human beings some pretty definite and unequivocal information that this was what he was doing? The Church seems to me to say that we can be sure that Jesus was God because a Council in the fourth century passed a resolution to that effect, be it said after some lively disagreement on the issue, and even under some crude pressure on some delegates. This is a rather questionable way for God to confirm to humankind such a momentous event as his arrival in the flesh on earth, and this confirmation came approximately three hundred years after the event.

That God uses the books of the Bible as a way of communicating with people is also strange. The best information we have on the central issues of Christianity comes from New Testament writings in which the contents are pretty selective and the whole collection is somewhat haphazard. Nonetheless we do get a clear picture of Jesus, his teaching and work, even though some of the information about Jesus in these writings is contradictory. For example he taught us to turn the other cheek, love our enemies, do good to those who despitefully use us, and yet he himself is recorded by the writer of St John's Gospel as having taken a whip and driven the traders and money-changers out of the Temple. It sounds as if rather than turn the other cheek he lost his temper.

We don't know who wrote many of the books of the Bible. Contrary to what the Church believed for more than fifteen hundred years scholars today, for good reasons, tell us that Moses didn't write the early books of the Old Testament and that Paul didn't, for example, write the Epistle to the Ephesians. The Catholic Church says that only the teaching magesterium of the Church has the authority to give an authentic interpretation of scripture. Protestants would say that the inspiration of scripture by God means that whatever you and I may think about its lack of precision, within certain parameters it is a communication from God.

It seems to me that it is a bit unfair of God that the Bible, as a piece of communication, is so diverse and hit and miss and fraught with internal critical problems. The writings contained in it were written by a great diversity of people in very different situations over a period of many years. With histories, prophesies, gospels and ordinary letters, theologians and churchmen authenticate doctrines on the flimsiest evidence of sometimes obscure or remote texts. They do it in such a way that the original writers, I have no doubt, would be scandalised that what they wrote was used in such a way. For example it is proposed that the foreshadowing of the doctrine of the Trinity can be seen in the appearance of three men to Abraham in an apparition, the threefold 'holy' in Isaiah's famous vision in the year that King Uzziah died and in the Spirit, the most High and the Son in the Annunciation, although not in the right order. All of these biblical texts were deemed at one time by theologians to support the doctrine of the Trinity. It seems that rather than God ordaining the Bible as his communication to humankind, humankind decided that it was so.

There is a theological principle that the late Harry McAdoo, former Church of Ireland Archbishop of Dublin, espoused at every possible opportunity, the principle of 'the faith once for all delivered to the saints'. It conjures up for me an image of a courier delivering a package to a group of saints gathered together in a room like at Pentecost. As I understand it the principle here is that God revealed the faith necessary for salvation by a certain point early on in the life of the Church, and that this body of faith was complete and immutable; that the Church cannot add to or take from it. I asked a lecturer in Anglicanism recently when this process was completed and he confessed he didn't know, but it probably ended with the final acceptance by the Church of the canon of the New Testament. How Harry knew that God had done this I don't know. The lecturer said he'd come back to me about it, and he never did. One thing I do know, however, is that Harry McAdoo used it to say that nobody since the delivery of the original body of faith can promulgate new doctrines and claim that they are necessary for salvation. I have a sneaking suspicion he had the Roman Catholic Church in mind!

At this point it seems that biblical scholars have mined everything possible from the texts of the Bible, and as R.M. Grant of the University of Chicago said, unless new sources are discovered there is really nothing more for scholars to say about the New Testament. One writer puts it: 'From beginning to end, the New Testament is caught up in mystery. Scholars will never solve its difficulties, though there is no harm in their trying. Glints of what the mystery was and is, are only discernible through worship.' That the Church has made the most of the documents it has, I do not doubt. Nor do I doubt the sincerity of those who believe that the findings of Councils of the Church are the truth about God. I do doubt that it is fair of God, if the initiative was his, to use such equivocal methods to communicate eternal truths to fallible human beings.

That God should have given his message to one small tribe in the Middle East at a particular time in history is also strange. It was hardly fair to all the Chinese and Indians and other residents of the then known world that they had to wait so long to hear it, and even then the success of Christian missionaries was patchy. Do you ever wonder what became of approximately half the apostles about whom, after Jesus' time, we heard nothing? I wonder where they got to, how they got on and if any of them gave up and went home. Of course America and Australia hadn't been discovered then, and surely to be fair God should have felt some responsibility for ensuring that the indigenous peoples of those countries had a chance in a reasonable amount of time to hear the message. They had to wait 1,500 or more years for colonisation by Christians who weren't, to say the least, very kind to them.

The other great problem, of course, is that since the times the books of the Bible were written and the essential doctrines of the Church were formulated, our knowledge of ourselves and the world we live in, has developed radically. For example our knowledge of science today, especially of physiology and psychology are bound to affect how we view the miracles. The writer of Matthew's account of Jesus healing the boy who often fell into the fire or into water describes him by using the Greek word for lunatic, while Mark says he had a dumb spirit and Luke simply says he had a spirit. The composite picture of the boy's malady from the three gospel accounts makes it look likely that he was an epileptic. If he were alive today he would be on medication. Is it possible that Lazarus wasn't dead at all, but in some kind of coma? Modern medicine may throw light on the healing miracles but doesn't undermine the purpose of the stories; that belief can help overcome physical illness, a view that modern medicine supports. I don't wish to downgrade the healings of Jesus, but neither do I want to suspend my reason when thinking about them. Our knowledge of astronomy today also challenges us with a different perspective on heaven, earth and hell than the simple three-decker universe the people of biblical times believed they lived in.

All these things can lead to fascinating explorations of the biblical accounts without necessarily undermining them completely. We view stories about virgin births, which were in the mythologies of other religions in the east at the time, miracles and resurrection and other religious phenomena differently today. We don't necessarily undermine their significance or meaning, but many people want to express significance and meaning in other than the simple miraculous terms that were credible at the time, but are not believable to many people today.

Whatever it was that overcame the disciples, it transformed them from being frightened and disillusioned men into a group with a message of love and forgiveness that when it is implemented can have a profound influence on people's lives. The truth of the resurrection is not provable from the events of the time. We can never know if the tomb was empty after the resurrection. I don't believe that faith in the resurrection depends on any theory about what happened to the body of Jesus. We cannot investigate those events historically. The truth of the resurrection is a present reality believed in faith by millions of people today. How it all came about we will never know. Some clergy don't like this kind of approach. They say that proper faith is only possible when people hold an unquestioning and unconditional commitment to the doctrines of the Church or the teachings of the Bible as they interpret them. Some people, however, feel they must adopt a questioning approach if Christianity is to remain credible to them in the twenty-first century.

For others the key to believing the truths of Christianity is to accept that religious language is metaphorical. One letter to *The Irish Times* (it's hard to escape the conclusion that my theology might be different if I took the *Irish Independent*), was a defence of Andrew Furlong. Andrew was forced to resign as rector from his Church of Ireland parish because, amongst other things, he did not believe in the divinity of Jesus. The letter said: 'To say "I believe in God" and that "Jesus is the son of God" can only be metaphorical – the means by which we try to say, on the one hand, that life is not exhausted by its physical and material limitations and on the other, that (to use other metaphorical language) "God was in Christ reconciling the world to himself." The biblical stories of the birth, death and resurrection of Jesus can only be extended metaphors through which realities that transcend the literal are expressed.'

I think I understand this and it makes sense to me, but did the early fathers of the Church when they laid down the Christolgical doctrines of the Church, understand religious language as metaphor? Did Popes, bishops and theologians throughout the centuries since, understand religious language in this way, and if not what are the implications of such a shift to metaphor for our understanding of orthodox Christian doctrine today? Again, over to the theologians. Of one thing I am sure that in thirty-three years in the ministry I don't believe I met more than a couple parishioners, if that, who would have understood the gospel accounts as other than literal and historical.

That Andrew Furlong, the Church of Ireland rector brought before an ecclesiastical court, had difficulties with traditional doctrines of the Christian faith is perfectly understandable in this day and age. Given that he denied the divinity of Jesus, and knowing the position of the Church of Ireland, it was unrealistic of him to have hoped that he could stay in the parochial ministry. In my view he should have resigned from his parish sooner than he did. I also believe, however, that his bishop was wrong to bring him before an ecclesiastical court to be tried for heresy after only a few months. If after a couple of years the difficulties between Andrew and his bishop could not have been resolved pastorally, as they appear to have been in the end, then an ecclesiastical court might have been considered. The undue haste with which a heresy trial was arranged was, I believe, a great mistake. Perhaps there were facts I did not know that might change this view, but I cannot think what they might be.

Epilogue

As I sat in the stillness of the sleepy reading room hidden behind the morning newspaper, absorbed in news from around the world, a reader near me shattered the silence with a lusty greeting to a new arrival, 'Hello, how are things in Botswana?' This violation of the quietness of the place disturbed my concentration, but amused me as I wondered how the new arrival, presumably recently home from that country, might answer such a general question. Was the questioner looking for information on the economy or even the weather? Was he enquiring for the family or perhaps about work? Were there recent political developments in Botswana into which he hoped to gain some up-to-date insight? I found the question all the more amusing since although I knew Botswana was somewhere in Africa, I could not place it on a map. As it turned out I did not hear how the recent arrival answered the question as, with more respect for other readers than the questioner, he said something quietly I could not hear.

Behind my paper I had come to the conclusion that it was impossible to give other than a polite meaningless generalisation in answer to the question without first asking a question in return. That is exactly the same as when a person asks: 'Do you believe in God?' A simple answer 'yes' or 'no', does not communicate anything of significance without first asking the questioner in return: 'What do you mean by God?' Does the questioner in the first place have an image of God as the man in the sky with flowing robes, a beard and a big book? Or does he have an image of God as the unknowable cause of the big bang, or a dozen possibilities between.

Traditional Christian theology says that God is both immanent and transcendent, immanent meaning dwelling within us, in the individual human being, and transcendent meaning beyond human knowledge. It is interesting to note that the dictionary definition of 'transcendent' also says 'abstrusely speculative'. I do not believe in a transcendent God. I haven't the remotest idea how the universe came into existence, but I'm prepared to accept the big bang scientific account of creation for the moment, despite the likelihood that a bright new generation of astrophysicists may come up with a conflicting theory next week.

It stretches my credulity too far to believe that a God, as most people understand the word, created the universe, unless you simply want to call whatever force caused the universe God, but then I don't think that's what traditional theology means by God. I believe in the immanence of love; where love is, God is, and where there is no love God is absent. The writer of the first Epistle of John says, 'Nobody has seen God at any time,' but 'if we love one another God dwells in us'. The writer also says; 'God is love and he that dwells in love dwells in God and God in him'. I no longer believe in a transcendent God.

I no longer believe in the supernatural or miraculous aspects of Jesus. I believe that Jesus was a historical figure who was an embodiment of love and taught and lived love to the point he was prepared to die for it and did. After his death his disciples believed they experienced him alive in some mysterious way, and fired by this love they went out to preach the good news to the world. The Church very soon largely ignored this love as it became obsessed with conformity to doctrinal definitions and the need to exercise control over people to enforce belief in these doctrines. The Church used fear as an instrument to impose a heaven-and-hell kind of salvation on credulous people. People who had a need to believe that there was more to life than just surviving or just not, and believed that there is an afterlife in which all the injustices of this world will be put right. I see love as salvation, but I do not believe that this salvation includes life after death. Salvation is achieved by living the most authentic human life possible here on earth and the means of doing that is self-giving, and often costly, love.

It is important to make the distinction between knowing something and believing it. Not the Pope, the Archbishop of Constantinople, the Archbishop of Canterbury nor anybody else knows that there is life after death. They believe it of course, but as faith implies doubt, they really ought to admit from time to time that they sometimes have doubts or may be wrong. Some people's faith is so strong that they talk about knowing something when in fact they believe it, and I understand that. I, personally, don't have a need to believe in life after death. I am quite content to think I will be extinct when I die. I would hate to live forever, in any state of being. Whatever about surviving in a blissful heaven, I would dread the thought that I might have to live another life in this world with its preponderance of evil, pain and suffering, which if I were a Buddhist I might have to believe. Naturally I wouldn't be too keen on the traditional Christian hell either, which is where, I have no doubt, some readers believe I will end up.

Of course I may be wrong about all my beliefs and opinions. Many of the issues upon which I have made up my own mind are issues that the theologians have dealt with and some have arrived at conclusions they can reconcile with orthodox Christianity. It is important to stress that my own conclusions are provisional. Future life experience may force me to change my mind. For example if I were diagnosed with a terminal illness tomorrow and given a week to live I might change my mind about life after death. I'm pretty certain I wouldn't, but I cannot know unless it were to happen. Furthermore I am not canvassing other people to agree with me; I am not trying to promote a point of view to which I want to convert other people. I simply want to say honestly what I believe.

Trying to summarise a version of the whole endeavour of Christian theology in a few chapters is impossible, but please remember that this is not a theological treatise but a memoir, a memoir of a life that started in Wexford almost seventy years ago. I've had a charmed life to date. I had thirty-three great years in the ministry of the Church of Ireland. I enjoyed it and cannot imagine having done anything else. Life has been a marvellous journey so far and although I haven't landed on the main runway I am enjoying immensely the rest of the trip.

It's a long way from Lizzie Meyler selling 'fresh herrinds' in the Bull Ring in Wexford to all of the theological matters I have mentioned and yet I have a feeling that Lizzie would have understood intuitively what it is I have been trying to say.